IN THE HANDS OF AN ANGRY

DEMIGOD

BIBLICAL HELP FOR ENGAGING
THE CHRONIC SELF-WORSHIPER

BRANDI HUERTA

In the Hands of an Angry Demigod: Biblical Help for Engaging the Chronic Self-Worshiper

Graphic design: Rachel Huerta

Cover photo by Brandi Huerta

Editor: Rachel Huerta

Editor: Maureen Beck

ISBN 9798338044483

https://www.facebook.com/brandi.huerta72/

For Matthew, Rachel, and Josiah, my greatest gifts on this earth. Thank you for your endless love, support, and friendship. You are tangible proof that God is good and that He gives good gifts to His children. I love you so very much.

And to my friends who have exemplified courage through the costly grace of God's providence: I cannot thank YHWH enough for the gift you are to me. I would wish you a happier life, but I would never rob you of the fruit God has granted you through your faithfulness to Him. He has been unspeakably kind to me through you.

CONTENTS

Introduction

At the end of twelve months he was walking on the roof of the royal palace of Babylon, and the king answered and said, "Is not this great Babylon, which I have built by my mighty power as a royal residence and for the glory of my majesty?" While the words were still in the king's mouth, there fell a voice from heaven, "O King Nebuchadnezzar, to you it is spoken: The kingdom has departed from you, and you shall be driven from among men, and your dwelling shall be with the beasts of the field. And you shall be made to eat grass like an ox, and seven periods of time shall pass over you, until you know that the Most High rules the kingdom of men and gives it to whom he will." Immediately the word was fulfilled against Nebuchadnezzar. He was driven from among men and ate grass like an ox, and his body was wet with the dew of heaven till his hair grew as long as eagles' feathers, and his nails were like birds' claws.

Daniel 4:29–33

When I was a kid, I was really good at spelling. I easily won my school spelling bee one year and advanced to the regional competition, where I sized up my opponents and surmised that there, too, I would have no trouble winning. As the other spellers fell away in the later rounds, I began telling the God I didn't truly know yet which of them I thought would be a good choice for second place and asking Him to bless them to that esteemed position. I wish I were making this up!

When it was down to me and one other competitor, I was given an easy word… one which I flubbed because, in my arrogance and complacency, my mind wasn't fully engaged, so I misspoke. I hurriedly corrected my error, but the damage was done. The judge shook her head sadly, and the girl—whose character and intellect were both greater than mine, as I later learned—spelled my word correctly, followed by another word, and won the bee.

I wish I could say I was humbled by that experience, but I wasn't. My pride was wounded, but I consoled myself that I *was* the best speller in the room, and if that judge had only had the compassion to recognize my honest mistake, I and not the other speller would have had my rightful place as victor.

The thing is, I *knew* in my heart of hearts why I lost the spelling bee, but I suppressed that knowledge in unrighteousness and quickly fabricated a story that was more flattering to me. I had been victimized, treated unfairly. My conscience—the God-given voice within me that is like a check engine light warning me of soul-danger—became just a bit more hardened as a result. It would be a few more years yet before God would intervene by regenerating me and initiating the years-long process of granting me truth in my inward parts. The Lord's convicting work in my life was far from over, and I am desperately thankful He didn't give up on me.

Several decades ago when this incident happened, self-esteem culture was alive and well. Friends and family who didn't want me to feel badly flattered me and pumped me up, probably from a sincere but dangerously flawed desire to love me well, and I was carried away and enticed—not by their words, but by my own sinful desire to be grand in my own eyes. Oh, wretched human that I am.

Now that my age starts with a five and I have walked with the Lord for many years, I know that my blessedness and joy depends on my conscience being clear before the Lord. That doesn't stop me from exalting myself, but when I do, I'm more apt to recognize the noise in my soul. I now know that peace and freedom are there for the asking (1 John 1:9) if I will humble myself and agree with God about what is going on in my selfish heart. My self-pity and self-justification after the spelling bee may have seemed normal, and indeed they are, but they are also wicked, motivated by the flesh and the devil, and they were deadly to my soul.

I don't remember the specific days after the spelling bee, but I do remember what I was like in general at that time. I can picture myself being sullen and pouty, and my mom doing everything she could to make me happy. While her efforts probably pleased me, I couldn't let up too much on my sulking because I wanted her to continue to make my happiness her responsibility. I was sinning against her and I knew that, too, but I wanted what I wanted too badly and so I ignored the growing turmoil in my conscience until I had to start quieting it with drugs and promiscuity.

I kept trying to make myself happy, but more and more, I just wanted to die. I had a tough childhood and I blamed that, my parents, the moon—everyone and everything else for my depression. Come to find out, my own self-absorption was the cause of it.

Then the LORD said to Cain, "Why are you angry? And why has your countenance fallen? "If you do well, will not your countenance be lifted up?"

Genesis 4:6-7a, NASB

Cain was like me in that he thought his biggest problems were his brother and the God who doesn't really reward those who seek Him like He says He does. God's issue with Cain had more to do with the absence of a broken spirit and a contrite heart than it did about what Cain offered God in sacrifice. Everything is God's anyway, and He doesn't need anything from us. Cain and I thought the world and the Lord *owed us,* and our countenances were fallen because of it. Our dispositions reflected the conditions of our souls.

My brotha from another motha and I aren't weird, though. On the contrary, we're pretty normal humans. In this book, I will help you explore your own conscience, and the image of the Living God whose glory in you will mean your joy and wholeness. Jesus Christ, God incarnate, was the only fully sane person to ever walk the earth, and only to the extent that you are filled with the fruit of His Spirit (love) will you be sane as well. King Nebuchadnezzar found this out the hard way when he did not see fit to acknowledge God or give Him praise, and then found himself eating grass as his humanity was effaced, giving way to the nature of a brute beast. Self-exaltation is the opposite of

Christlikeness, and therefore the opposite of sanity, joy, and freedom as well.

An excellent and popular biblical counseling book suggests that other people are too big in our eyes, and that is the source of many of our soul problems. Contra that idea, I would say that the real issue is that we esteem ourselves too highly, and we expect others to do the same. To the extent that this is the case, we lack experiential peace.

If I'm right, soul care is not as complicated as you or I may have thought it was. If you have turmoil in your soul, literally all you have to do is to explore with God the ways you are exalting yourself, the ways you are not loving Him and others. If you are deeply habituated in self-centeredness, pervasive peace may take some time to attain, but with humility and perseverance you can begin to enjoy a measure of joy and freedom right away. You probably will need the help of people who see you more clearly than you see yourself, especially at the beginning of this new leg of your journey, but if you want to love God and glorify Him more than anything else, the Lord will bless you tremendously and, by the power of the Spirit, you will be able to do much of the heavy lifting on your own. While not everyone has a thriving soul care community, every Christian has everything they need for life and godliness, by God's kindness.

The posture of your heart will determine how you receive what I have shared so far. If you are either offended or unmoved because of a hard heart, you may be tempted to double down on your skewed view of yourself, the people in your life, and the world around you. If this is the case, the condition of your inward man will go from bad to worse. You will be further entrenched in a prison of your own making. May I encourage you to keep reading, and to prayerfully ask God to give you eyes to see, ears to hear, and a heart that understands how to love Him more, reflect Him better, and to consider others as being more significant than yourself? Oh how blessed you will be, Friend, if you do. May the Lord make much of Himself through you as you worship Him in spirit and in truth, and are consequently filled with His image and glory.

If, in reading this, you find that you heartily agree with what I'm saying, wishing you could get *that one person* to read it, will you fervently ask the Lord, however you see yourself, to grant you spiritual sight and a tender heart? While a person is alive and the eternal gospel exists, we hold out hope for everyone to change, grow, and see. Still, though, there comes a time for many when God gives them over to the hardness of their hearts. Don't assume this could not happen to you.

If God has given you a tender heart, but someone in your life has spiritual sensory malfunction, I pray the Lord will use this book to help you endure and to bring practical help to those around you. Always, always look to the log in your eye first, but then do not neglect to help others see theirs clearly. The other person may or may not change in the process, but the Lord asks only for your faithfulness to Him and to them while you wait on Him to bring transformation as He sees fit. He will mature you, grant you fruit, and give you Himself in ways you could never have imagined if you choose to trust Him, walking in faith and courage. Are you in?

1

Who is God

"What people revere, they resemble, either for ruin or restoration."

GK Beale

In his book *We Become What We Worship: A Biblical Theology of Idolatry,* GK Beale develops his observation that in Scripture, when people worship the Lord in spirit and in truth, they are transformed into His image, from one level of glory to another. Conversely, when they worship idols, they look like a creature rather than the Creator they were designed to reflect—a beast, instead of an image bearer of the true and living God.

The idols of the nations are nothing but silver and
gold,
The work of human hands.

They have mouths, but they do not speak;
They have eyes, but they do not see;
They have ears, but they do not hear,
Nor is there any breath at all in their mouths.
Those who make them will become like them,
Yes, everyone who trusts in them.

Psalm 135:15-18

Beale contends that *sensory malfunction language* (eyes that don't see, ears that don't hear, etc.) is describing but one effect of idolatry, and spiritual deformity of all sorts can only result from worship of anything that is not God. In this work, I will assume rather than try to prove what Dr. Beale has already said, and I recommend his excellent book to you for further study on the topic.

It should be evident, though, that to know God thoroughly and to love Him completely is the only path to spiritual wholeness and blessedness. Since knowing and loving are so closely related—you can't love what you don't know—we will endeavor here to place special emphasis on certain aspects of God's person and character. This book is not meant to be a comprehensive treatment of the doctrine of God, but everything we say must be grounded in Him or we will be left with only so much moralism and behavior modification. Thus, theology proper will play a prominent role in our discussion. God's very image, the image that was effaced in the Fall, must be restored in you. You must behold (and adore) so you can become.

Assuming you are regenerated, when God saved you, He declared you perfectly righteous by virtue of your union with Christ. The theological word for this declaration is *justification.* God does not make you practically perfect right away, though. Once you are saved, you spend the rest of your Christian life growing in your sanctification, which means that you are changing to resemble the God you increasingly revere. Hence you are both already and not yet righteous, and in a sense you are becoming what you already are.

Justification is monergistic, which means that God and God alone accomplishes it without any aid whatsoever from us. Sanctification, though, is synergistic, meaning that both God and we contribute to it. Your efforts really do matter, even though both the power and the will to change ultimately come from God. The result of this is that not all Christians grow to the same degree or reach the same level of maturity, and many genuine believers waste their time pursuing lesser things rather than running after God with all they are, to their own spiritual detriment *and* to the detriment of the church that is robbed of the fruit they would have borne. There is not much sadder, in my view, than an older saint without much fruit to show for their years of walking with the Lord.

Do you realize, Christian, that you will spend eternity growing in your knowledge of and love for God? There is no last thing about Him to be grasped; He is infinite and inexhaustible, and you will spend the rest of your unending existence further delighting in Him, if you truly belong to Him. In light of this, I have to ask you: do you pursue ever-deepening knowledge of Him now? I'm always surprised at how many Christians don't study theology. If you don't have a hunger to know God now, what makes you think you will enjoy heaven? At the very least, your lack of longing to know God points to spiritual sensory malfunction resulting from some degree of idolatry. The worst-case scenario is that you don't truly know Him at all.

I am good, and I do good. For me and to me are all things.
I require satisfaction when I am offended, according to my own standards of what an offense is. I have the right to decide.
My supposed "sins" are inconsequential.
There is no small sin against an immense god.
YHWH

I originally drew the graphic on this page for a counselee, and it came to inspire this book as I continued to think about its implications. The lady I was counseling found herself to be endlessly fascinating and important, and other people seemed to her to be bit players in the drama of which she was the star. YHWH Himself had but a supporting role. She would not have admitted this and didn't even recognize it. She persistently and consistently felt entitled that others serve her, and she was spiritually deformed, deaf and blind, as a result.

I drew her as the large, three-headed person on the left. She reminded me of a Greek goddess, of the kind that might have a mood swing today and smite you if you displeased her, and each of the heads represented her rapidly changing disposition in response to the people and circumstances whose service she demanded. If she gets what she wants, she's happy. If she doesn't… well, there's a lightning bolt in store for the offender. Since she is so important and wonderful, she doesn't see a problem with her behavior.

My pastor was in the room during the counseling session. He's a humble man, and made the sober observation that he's frequently like the god in the picture. I am as well. Until the eternal state when we are glorified, this will be the case to some degree—hopefully less and less as time goes on. If you're reading this book and you experience the kindness of God's conviction in your soul, turn from your selfishness and worship God. The promise of 1 John 1:9 is yours.

If we confess our sins, He is faithful and just to forgive us our sins and to cleanse us from all unrighteousness.

That promise is to the justified person: the person who, like Peter, is clean and needs only for his feet to be washed. Your sin can't remove your status as God's child, but it can steal your blessings and put a barrier between you and God, and between you and those around you as well. The "if" tells you that the promise is conditional, though: you must say what God says about your sin. If you snarl at someone because they inconvenience you, don't blame-shift and say that you're hangry or something else that removes the full responsibility from you. Nothing can come out of you but what was in you to begin with. The truth is that you have elevated yourself over another image-bearer and murdered him in your heart, per Jesus's words in Matthew 5:22. Your forgiveness and cleansing are dependent upon you saying the same thing God does about what's going on in your heart.

The friend I was counseling couldn't quite get there, couldn't quite agree with God about her sin, and so as I am writing this, she remains a deeply marred image bearer. In what ways does she resemble a false god rather than YHWH? What would change if she repented?

From Him and through Him and to Him are all things: God's aseity

God having all life, glory, goodness, blessedness, in and of himself: is alone in, and unto himself all-sufficient, not standing in need of any creature which he hath made, nor deriving any glory from them, but only manifesting his own glory in, by, unto, and upon them, his is the alone fountain of all Being, of whom, through whom, and to whom are all things…

From the Second London Baptist Confession of Faith, 2.2

Matthew Barrett says in None Greater[1]:

> *To affirm God's aseity is to say, first and foremost, that he is life in and of himself, and on that basis he must be self-existent and self-sufficient. It is because God is life in and of himself that there can be no sense in which he is caused by another.*

To be a creature is to derive existence from another, namely God. God is the only one who exists of Himself; the word *aseity* comes from the Latin phrase *a se,* meaning of or from one's self. He is the be all, end all. When a person acts as if she and not God has that position, as if she is the standard for all things and everyone answers to her, ironically,

---

[1] Barrett, Matthew. *None Greater: The Undomesticated Attributes of God.* Baker Books, 2019. p 56

she will be eminently dependent upon others as her sense of well-being will hang on people's recognition and approval of her. She worships a creature, namely herself, instead of YHWH. In seeking to obtain glory that belongs only to God, she becomes like a petulant, moody minor deity whose emotions are dictated by people and circumstances over which she has no control. Like all idolators, she is spiritually malformed.

The worshiper whose gaze has been captured by the *a se* God, though, has an otherworldly stability. To be a creature is to be caused and needy by definition, but the beholder of YHWH becomes steadfast and immovable, relatively unaffected by the sins and failures of others or the unpredictability of circumstances. He is satisfied with the Lord as his utterly sufficient source and so is not dependent on others for his happiness. He doesn't demand to be the god of his own little world, and he doesn't need people's applause, which frees him up to serve them.

Think about this: if you need people's approval too much, your integrity will always be for sale. You won't bring needed correction to others because you know you will risk their frowns if you do. You won't seek their input, either, because you are too big—you think highly of yourself and can't bear that other folks would think any less of you. Flattery, which comes from a lying tongue, becomes the rule of the day.

In that case the LORD, who is truth itself, is displaced from His rightful throne in your life as your image goes toward decay rather than wholeness and blessedness. The peace and joy that are your birthright will be elusive or altogether absent from your Christian experience.

The lack of truth in your inward parts will manifest itself in soul noise, which you will seek to quiet by any number of artificial means. Drugs, alcohol, sex, distractions, or endorphins can all grant temporary and false peace, respite from a screaming conscience.

How is your soul today, Friend?

Not a man that He would change His mind: God's impassibility

We are told in Scripture both that God changes His mind, and that He cannot change His mind. We read that there is no shadow in Him due to turning, and that He can be grieved and angered. How are we to make sense of these seeming contradictions, and why does the Word describe our Lord in these ways?

The answer is similar to the way we reconcile the verses that tell us God is spirit, without a body, and the ones that tell us He has hands and eyes. The expressions that attribute human physical characteristics to God are called *anthropomorphisms,* and when we read them, we fairly naturally understand that they communicate something true about God without *being* true of Him, properly speaking. When the Bible tells us that the Lord hides us in the shadow of His wing, we understand that it speaks of His omnipotent, unwavering care and protection of His people, and not of His chicken-like form (when animal characteristics are applied to God, it's called a *zoomorphism*).

When a human emotion is predicated of God, it's called an *anthropopathism,* and should no more be taken literally than an anthropomorphism or a zoomorphism should. Theologians have said that YHWH is the "most blessed," and that He dwells in happy repose. Both of these statements reflect

God's absolute perfection. Any sadness or anger actually existing in Him would indicate a diminishment of His perfection of blessedness, which cannot be the case.

When the Lord is said to be angry or grieved in response to sin, understand that the lack of perfection is in the creature, and the way that creature experiences God in that moment is that the Lord's perfect goodness and justice is causing the creature to suffer. God has not changed or moved in any way. He cannot. And God can never come upon new information that causes Him to adjust His course in the slightest, regretting or repenting in the way we do.

The point of connection is not between the emotional state of a human that repents and some emotional state in God, but in the action taken. When someone repents, they stop doing what they were doing, and they begin to do something else. So also, God created man, then he destroyed man, God made Saul king, then he removed him, and God threatened judgment on Nineveh, then he removed the sentence of judgment. You can call that repentance because of the analogy between God's action and human actions, without taking along with it the baggage of human emotional turmoil. When we repent, it is because something confronts us and we are changed. Spiritually speaking, we turn from sin to righteousness. Generally speaking, we encounter some problem, we regret a decision, and we redo something, or start over, or do something else. God's existence is not bound by time. Quite to the contrary, God has foreordained whatsoever comes to pass, and he accomplishes all his holy will. So can a simple spiritual God who has decreed all things and cannot be hindered, can that God repent? Not in the sense that we do. But did he decree from all eternity both to create man, and to destroy him, to make Saul king, and then to remove him, to threaten Nineveh, and then to deliver it? Absolutely. And those actions are described to us in human language.

Samuel Renihan[2]

Jesus—God in human flesh—experiences human emotion because He was and is human, but His divine nature undergoes no emotional change whatsoever. His human emotions, though, do give us some cues as to how a Christian can in some

[2] Renihan, Samuel. *God Without Passions: A Primer.* RBAP, 2015. p 28

measure reflect the impassible God. Jesus rejoiced at the things that honored the Father, and grieved at the things that dishonored Him. He was not controlled by people and circumstances, but remained singularly focused on doing the will of the Father. Betrayal by enemies, friends, and family and relentless persecution from Satan and his minions did not dissuade Him in the slightest from His mission. The goal and trajectory of the Christian's life should always be to become more like the Lord in this way.

Think about the too-big person in the previous graphic: anything and everything has the power to throw her if it doesn't go her way. In fact, literally *nothing at all* has the power to throw her. Recall Proverbs 28:1, which says that the wicked runs when no one pursues them. This is true, not only of unbelievers, but of believers as well. A person who thinks too highly of herself frequently thinks she's being persecuted when she isn't, and can often experience intense fear, even when there is no external perceived threat (we'll talk about that more in the next chapter). What she reveres (the earthly, the creaturely, the moveable) is what she resembles, for ruin and not for restoration.

For this reason, as we discuss how to change and how to help other people change, impassibility will be of the utmost importance to our thinking.

God without parts: divine simplicity

The nature of God has been revealed to us in a myriad of created effects because no one creaturely concept can contain or explain Him. In our minds, there are distinctions among what we call the attributes of God, but in Him, they all are identical with Him and with one another. Some theologians refer to these as *perfections* and wisely say that God *is* His perfections, rather than expressing that He possesses attributes, in order to communicate this truth more clearly. If love were something that existed apart from God, or as *a* part of Him, He would be dependent on it in some measure to be what He is. He is not *loving;* He *is* love itself. He *is* wisdom. Conceptually, those things are distinct to us. In truth, they are simply God's nature expressed in ways we, as creatures composed of parts, can comprehend. Composite creatures have composite thoughts, and no one human idea (or even all of the human ideas combined!) can come close to communicating who and what the simple God is.

One vital application of this truth as it pertains to our discussion is that, even as a composite image-bearer of the simple God, you can't have peace if you don't have love, and vice versa. Again, those two attributes and facets of the fruit of the Spirit are conceptually distinct to us, but their substance is identical because originally they both are equal to God, and only faintly modeled in us.

Further, God does not have any unrealized potential as one of His "parts." A sunflower seed has the potential to be a sunflower, which it may or may not achieve, but you do not have that attribute as part of who or what you are. The sunflower doesn't have the potential to be an accountant, which you may have (I sure don't!). Potential is not the kind of part you can see or feel, but it exists nonetheless, or else you could never become what you currently are not. God is perfect—He is all Being, with no becoming. Because of His simplicity, He is not even capable of change of any sort, from within or without. This means that He can't change Himself and He can't be changed by anything or anyone else. You can't "make" Him sad because He can only be what He is, which is absolute blessedness itself. As you revere and resemble Him, you will experience the fullness of blessing not otherwise available to a fallen creature.

Another way to consider God's simplicity is to say that He is *actus purus,* or pure act, with no passive potency. This means that He is the cause of everything that is not Him, and nothing causes Him to be in any way. Nothing happens to God. Because of this, He cannot be victimized. It's just not possible. Have you ever felt sorry for God because His children disobey Him so, or sorry that He had to watch His one and only Son die? You shouldn't think of God in this way. Yes, the sin of the world should grieve you appropriately, and you should long for and pursue what glorifies God. But do not see Him as a victim.

Because of this, you shouldn't see yourself as a victim, either. Everything that happens to you is according to God's single, undivided plan, which is absolutely perfect. He does nothing but good because He can't act contrarily to His nature. His plan is singular, even though it works out in a myriad of created effects. Time is a creation, an environment for creatures, and it unfolds for us successively. God, however, simply *is.* There is nothing accessible to Him only as a memory, and there's nothing He looks forward to, because all of His life is a simultaneous now.

God's eternity is the whole, simultaneous, and perfect possession of boundless life.

Boethius

Eternity is contrary to time and is, therefore, a permanent and immutable state; a perfect possession of life without any variation. As the nature of time consists in the succession of parts, so the nature of eternity is an infinite immutable duration.

Stephen Charnock[3]

If you see yourself as a passive victim to your circumstances, you will be miserable. If you see your life as a gift from God, though, and *act* consistently and faithfully to your Scripture-

---

[3] Charnock. *The Existence and Attributes of God.* 1:280

revealed responsibilities before Him, you will find joy and fulfillment.

As a further implication of this idea, don't make a habit of doing for someone what they can do for themselves. Teach them, lead them by example, and hold their arms up so they have the strength to fight, but don't encourage passivity in them by helping them neglect their responsibilities. Many folks want their problems to go away more than they want to grow, and they want the blame for any failure to lie with someone else. Some have been made to feel powerless and worthless, and helping them find their God-given strength is the greatest gift you can give them. As a general rule, don't pursue them in order to help them. Requiring them to reach out to you gives them agency, and helps them fulfill their responsibility to work out their own salvation. Your goal should be to help people not to need you.

There will be times when you should and must fight for people or defend them, but those times are relatively rare. They must learn to depend on the Word and the Spirit themselves and grow in wisdom. A person can't gain wisdom without acting, making mistakes, learning, repenting when necessary, and repeating all of this over and over. Taking these things from folks ensures they will stay in spiritual infancy forever, not growing into the image of the God who is pure act. If you need people to need you, you may well be a demigod, and you and your followers will be spiritually malformed.

I would encourage you to explore the works I quoted in this chapter to help you gaze upon the beauty of God, that He may get the glory He's due and that you may bear His image, to the healing of your soul.

Behold Him, Believer. The more that the Lord, the Giver of light, becomes your focus and the light by which you see everything and everyone else, what could possibly shake you? In the pages to follow, we will look at some specific ways that people become too big in their own eyes, reaping spiritual malformation, and consider how they may be restored to joy and blessedness through loving God and loving others.

2

How Your Conscience Works

Alimony, alimony paying for your bills. When your conscience hits, you knock it back with pills.

Led Zeppelin

Now, Watergate does not bother me. Does your conscience bother you? Tell the truth.

Lynyrd Skynyrd

So it came about in the course of time that Cain brought an offering to the LORD of the fruit of the ground. Abel on his part also brought of the firstlings of his flock and of their fat portions. And the LORD had regard for Abel and for his offering; but for Cain and for his offering He had no regard. So Cain became very angry and his countenance fell. Then the LORD said to Cain, "Why are you angry? And why has your countenance fallen? If you do well, will not your countenance be lifted up? And if you do not do well, sin is crouching at the door; and its desire is for you, but you must master it."

Genesis 4:3-7

Every way of a man is right in his own eyes, but the LORD weighs the heart.

Proverbs 21:2

You were made to reflect the glory of God, and you do this when you love God and love others. When you aren't doing this well, your Maker gave you a blessed internal warning system called the conscience to alert you that something isn't right in your heart. Since each of us tends to justify our sinful behavior, blame it on God and others, or deny it altogether, our testimonies about our own motives aren't always trustworthy. God's gracious gift of an internal witness to His truth is the spiritual version of physical pain receptors, warning us through the means of discomfort that we need to take action of some kind.

The word "conscience" comes from a Latin phrase meaning "with knowledge"; you probably know the Bible teaches that every person is without excuse when they sin against God. (Romans 1:18-20, 2:14-15). They simply cannot *not* know that He exists and that He requires their obedience. This is much truer for the believer who has the added blessing of the indwelling Holy Spirit, on top of the conscience given as a common grace to every person. For this reason, even though believers (should) sin less than the world does, when they do sin, often their resultant soul noise is much louder than an unbeliever's would be.

A person's conscience doesn't always work as well as it should, however. When we ignore our consciences, they can become hardened and much less receptive to the Spirit's conviction (they don't bark when they should). Also, your conscience can be weak, meaning that it barks when it shouldn't, as when you think something's a sin when it's not. See 1 Corinthians 8:1-13 for one such instance.

You should always seek to conform your conscience to the teaching of Scripture, keeping well in mind that even though something is ok for you to do, it may not be wise for you—like drinking if you struggled with drunkenness in the past, or listening to a certain kind of music if it draws you back into your before-Christ former manner of thinking. (Note that this doesn't mean your brother or sister can't drink a glass of wine or listen to that song that trips you up; you can't make your convictions normative for everyone.)

As you are recalibrating your conscience, you will want to tread lightly. It's never wise to disobey your conscience unless you have clear testimony from Scripture that you have been living under a yoke that is not yours to bear. In the meantime, if you are convinced something is a sin for you, then it's a sin and you are not free to engage in the behavior in question. If you have come to see that you have a weak conscience in a particular matter, you may choose to begin to exercise your liberty in that area, *provided that you love God and others as you do so.*

Consider, for example, that you were raised to believe wearing denim to church is a sin, but you now know the Bible carries no such prohibition. If you choose now to wear denim to church, you would want to do so in humility toward others. Drinking alcohol and other freedoms carry with them the possibility that someone else may fall back into what truly is sin for them if you do not exercise your liberty with grace and discretion. When you love God and others, nothing is ever primarily about you, although you can and should keep in mind that God has given you all good things to enjoy.

Having said that, it's not always loving to cater to the weakest conscience in the room. It's wrong to offend people for the sake of offending them, but it's not always wrong to enjoy liberties you know will be upsetting to some folks. Again, humility is the key. Sometimes challenging others' convictions can keep them from forcing their unbiblical ideas on others, thereby unnecessarily complicating the souls of immature believers.

Loving God and others means doing the best you can to act in the best interests of other people, making much of God's name and fame, especially when no one is watching. Are you proud of your superior spiritual knowledge or morality? How do you treat those who differ with you? If a brother or sister genuinely is sinning in their practice of Christian liberty, are you willing to correct them with courage, compassion, and humility?

Loving people is not so much about your behavior as it is about the motive for your behavior. Rule keepers want to know what they should *do.* Give them a list and they're happy. Lists are easy and manageable, and when they check off every item (or at least most of them—nobody's perfect, after all!), they can look down smugly and expectantly on the others who are not measuring up. On the other hand, people-pleasers do what they do for applause, so that they don't care about being holy as much as they value being perceived as being holy. Both of these approaches to behavior are self-seeking, and all of us do them to some degree. Will you take some time to prayerfully contemplate what I've just said and ask the Lord to help you see your motives toward others clearly? What needs to change in your heart? The Lord has called you and every Christian to serve the church through loving correction, and He has called you to examine yourself first. If this is the practice and pattern of your life, please don't neglect to bring care to others and help them see their own motives clearly.

It can be tricky to discern people's motives, and in general it's best to take folks at their word. The problem with this, of course, is that the heart is deceitful above all things. People lie to one another, and they lie to themselves, sometimes to the point where they actually believe the lies to varying degrees. If you only ever believe people's self-testimonies, you will be a naïve and ineffective soul care provider. If you only ever disbelieve people's self-testimonies, you will be bitter, cynical, and angry, and you won't spread God's fame, except in the sense that all things—even evil ones—glorify God. God doesn't share His omniscience with His creatures, but He does share wisdom, and it's there for the asking. Keep asking Him for it and don't let up. People will show you who they are over time, if you have the eyes to see what they are clearly putting on display.

If you want to be good at soul care, put your phone down and pay attention to people. When they ask how you are, answer them truly, graciously, and succinctly, and learn to ask them good questions in return. "How's your soul?" is a good one; people rarely ask what is meant by the question, and their answers are windows into their hearts. Even a simple question about what were the best and worst parts of a person's day can lead to wonderful insight into what motivates them and what they live for. Don't feel the constant need to correct everything they say, or even anything at all. Cultivate the skill of observation.

For the people with whom you have the privilege of living in community, watch their behavior over a long period of time. Do their words and actions match?

Do the people around you claim to be full of love, but disdain doing menial tasks for other people? Are they genuinely servant-hearted, or do they direct most of their efforts toward those they want to impress? If they discern your and others' thoughts well, watch them over time to try to see whether it's because they love people and think deeply about them, or because they are always reading their approval ratings in the countenances of others. Do they listen more than they talk? Do they consistently and joyfully give credit where credit is due? Do they listen well and encourage people to open up only so that they can store the information they gain for future use? How do they take correction? How do they give correction? *Do* they give correction at all?

You should also be watching folks (yourself included—please go back through the questions and answer them for yourself) to get a sense of how quiet or noisy their souls are. If their words are false and don't truly reflect their hearts, even if they do a good job maintaining a semblance of public consistency, the person will exhibit soul noise, or a lack of experiential peace. Recall our discussion in the last chapter: God's perfections are equal with Himself and with one another, so that if a person isn't truthful and/or loving, they can't have peace either, because they aren't reflecting the God who is identical with all of those characteristics. The simple God reveals Himself in a myriad of created effects. As we humans contemplate creation, we do distinguish between, say, love and wisdom; in reality, in God, they are the same. Because of this, a person can only be wise to the extent that he or she is loving, and can only be at peace to the extent that he or she is truthful. If a person is in turmoil, understand that something likely is wrong in his conscience.

Here are some verses for you to consider. Together they provide the Scriptural basis for our discussion on soul noise, sometimes called conscience sorrow:

The wicked flee when no one is pursuing, but the righteous are bold as a lion.

Proverbs 28:1

If our heart does not condemn us, we have confidence before God.

1 John 3:21

There is no fear in love, but perfect love casts out fear. For fear has to do with punishment, and whoever fears has not been perfected in love.

1 John 4:18

In his book *Self-Esteem, Self-Image, Self-Love: How to Trade the Trinity of Self-Worship for the Triangle of Self-Evaluation,* Nicolas Ellen says:

> *People or circumstances cannot produce conscience sorrow or conscience joy within you. You cannot produce conscience joy or conscience sorrow in*

> *yourself or a confidence before God or lack of confidence before God. These feelings are by-products of your thoughts, words, and actions. If you are thinking, speaking, acting, or reacting in sinful ways toward God, people, or circumstances, you can expect conscience sorrow and a lack of confidence before God. If you are thinking, speaking, acting, or reacting in godly ways toward God, people, and circumstances, you can expect conscience joy and confidence before God.*

It would be well worth your time to read *The Heart of Man and the Mental Disorders: How the Word of God is Sufficient,* by Rich Thomson. Rich Thomson mentored Nicolas Ellen regarding the conscience, and his book is a masterful treatment of the subject. Part 1 treats the biblical theology of the conscience, while part 2 serves as reference material instructing on how conscience issues manifest in the form of various mental illnesses. It's a long, though not overly technical, and extremely fascinating read. Any believer can grow and change, and can do much to counsel others, using this book alone.

Consider Proverbs 28:1 again. "The wicked" doesn't just refer to the worst of the worst unregenerate people; the verse also applies to any of us when we have an unloving attitude toward God and/or others. Fleeing when no one is pursuing or running when no one is chasing you looks like any fear when there is no external perceived threat, or fear that is disproportionate to the threat. It can be as small and simple as getting defensive when someone asks an innocent question, or as large and overwhelming as a genuine believer's terror that God is ready to smite her and throw her into hell. No amount of gospel comfort will suffice when the problem is internal and subjective, as in when the soul's disquiet has been produced by unrepentant ungodly anger toward someone, or frustration that God is not running His universe properly. Both of these conditions arise from a "too big" person, per our previous illustration, earning the opposition of God (James 4:6). Humble people see themselves rightly, consider others to be more significant than themselves, and honor the Lord supremely. These are the folks with experiential peace from God—quiet souls. They have the peace that passes understanding, meaning that the state of their souls seems incongruous with the chaos that sometimes surrounds them.

Anxiety, paranoia, hypochondria, and hopelessness are but a few ways we can run when no one is chasing us. Ponder each of those terms and see if you can see why I said that. It would be good for you to continually ask the Lord to help you see more ways this can happen, so you can see them as check engine lights for the soul that lead you to run a spiritual diagnostic. Another class of behaviors that should raise your soul care antennae is alleviation behaviors, which are artificial ways of producing a quiet soul. If you can't or won't run to Christ for cleansing, you will need to find conscience relief somehow. Drugs and alcohol provide temporary artificial peace, as do sex, drugs, binge watching or scrolling, approval seeking (possibly relentlessly pursuing leadership positions), overeating, fantasizing… the list goes on. Many alleviation behaviors are not sinful in themselves, but train yourself to be alert to patterns of gravitating toward spiritual anesthesia.

When I was first learning to recognize my own soul noise, sometimes the sinful source was a mystery to me. It still is at times. The "engine diagnostic tool" I often use to figure out what is going on in my heart is 1 Corinthians 13:4-7, except that when I read it, I insert my name in the place of the word "love:" Brandi is patient, Brandi is kind… Brandi is not arrogant or rude…" etc. Generally speaking, at some point my conscience won't let me say the words out loud and I know where the problem lies.

Maybe I'm looking down on someone, thinking they're a worse sinner than I am. Maybe I see their sin rightly, but I don't want the hassle of obeying God's Galatians 6:1-2 command to restore them. Maybe my temper silently flared when they inconvenienced me, and now I'm guilty of murder at heart, according to Jesus. Now that I know what my problem is, freedom and joy are mine through the promise of 1 John 1:9. We talked about it in the previous chapter, but here it is again:

> *If we confess our sins, he is faithful and just to forgive us our sins and to cleanse us from all unrighteousness.*

If I call my sin what God calls it, ask Him for forgiveness and help, and believe the Lord's Word that my sin is taken away by the shed blood of Jesus, He will restore my soul. If my peace does not return, I know there's more work to do.

The second half of Proverbs 28:1, the running when no one is chasing verse, contrasts the righteous with the fleeing wicked person and says he is as bold as a lion. A clear conscience leads to courage, which is what you need to help a self-preferring, demigod type person. If you won't deal with your own unloving attitudes, you won't have the needed fortitude to serve a mini-god with patience, strength, and grace. It will take longer to help them than you will be able to endure. A lack of courage is a check engine light.

The great news is that the more you know how to deal with your own soul noise or conscience sorrow, the easier it will be to spot it in others. In many cases, you will have insight into people they don't have themselves. Again, linger long over observing people, asking good questions, thinking about them, and praying for them, and God will open your eyes and ears to things you never would have thought possible. Spiritual sensory malfunction, as we learned earlier, belongs to idolators. How is your sight today? How's your courage?

3

How to Think About Too-Big People

Special treatment for the special boy! Isn't that what you wanted?

Ginarrbrik to Edmund, in the movie version of *The Lion, the Witch, and the Wardrobe* by CS Lewis

...and in Hades, being in torment, he lifted up his eyes and saw Abraham far off and Lazarus at his side. And he called out, 'Father Abraham, have mercy on me, and send Lazarus to dip the end of his finger in water and cool my tongue, for I am in anguish in this flame.'

Luke 16:23–24

Too-big people are convinced of their own exceptionality and entitlement. Their views are right, their desires are right, and others should do what they want them to do. This statement is simplistic and it can work out in various ways and to various degrees, but it's generally true.

People often ask how these folks came to be the way they are. Some of them were mistreated earlier in life and rightly came to know they didn't deserve what was happening, so they determined they would never again allow themselves to be seen as less than. Others were treated as if they were the bright sun around which all the planets in the universe revolved, and they never questioned the truth of that assumption. Still others had one selfish, cruel parent, while the other parent tried to overcompensate for the harshness they endured by trying feverishly to build up what had been torn down in their precious child. None of these things may be true of the person you have in mind, though. Humans truly don't need any external influence in order to be self-absorbed; ever since our father and representative Adam fell, we—collectively—have been, as Martin Luther said, curved inward on ourselves.

> *Our nature, by the corruption of the first sin [being] so deeply curved in on itself that it not only bends the best gifts of God towards itself and enjoys them (as is plain in the works-righteous and hypocrites), or rather even uses God himself in order to attain these gifts, but it also fails to*

realize that it so wickedly, curvedly, and viciously seeks all things, even God, for its own sake.

Still, in a very true sense, how could someone raised in one of these ways have known how to be otherwise? As you seek to help hurting folks, you must hold two truths in tension and bring them to bear with wisdom: the person in front of you may have had tremendously difficult shaping influences to overcome, and they also know full well that there's a God against whom they are rebelling. If you forget either of these things, it will be difficult for you to be a redemptive influence on them. What's more, you are no more deserving of God's mercy and grace than they are. If you elevate yourself above them, you will disqualify yourself from helping them.

The kind of person we are talking about sees you as the small person at the end of the line, the dark one in the graphic. Your secret weapon is that you agree with them, as far as that goes, because you think biblically about yourself. You will necessarily disagree with their assessment that everything is about *them*—everything is for the Lord and His glory—but you know it's not about *you*, either. If you are content to be talked down to, mistreated, misunderstood, because you know your identity is firmly rooted in Christ, God will make much of Himself through you and bless you in the process as you minister. Understand that faithfulness and not the person's change is your responsibility. It will be easier to be faithful if you continually bear in mind that what the person says and does to you is not ultimately your fault. They have a sinful, selfish heart (like you do, like I do) and whoever gets near them gets splashed on, so to speak. If you are willing to be mistreated for the sake of Christ, not to return evil for evil, and to wisely look out for the person's best interest, you're in a good place to begin helping them. It goes without saying that this will be tremendously difficult, but I still want to acknowledge that fact.

Having a quiet, sturdy soul is absolutely crucial to your efforts because the folks we're talking about use their anger—even if the anger comes out through pitiful tears or huffing under breath instead of yelling—to control others, and most people won't stand up to them because it's easier not to. When this happens, it reinforces the all-about-me worldview of the one who desperately needs the help he is not getting.

Do you remember Isaiah chapter 6? Isaiah saw the pre-incarnate Christ (John 12:41) and then, as RC Sproul[4] said, Isaiah saw Isaiah for the first time. This led to the holiest man in Israel pronouncing a woe on himself because of his own filthiness. It also led to his acceptance of YHWH's mission without asking what it entailed, a mission on which the Lord promised to harden Isaiah's hearers so they would not repent and would ruthlessly persecute the messenger. Isaiah became what he beheld. A glimpse of the holiness, goodness, and beauty of Christ granted him the stability he needed for one of the most difficult ministries imaginable. This is why I encouraged you, dear reader, to immerse yourself in the study of the

[4] Sproul, RC. *The Holiness of God.* Tyndale, 1985, 1998. Chapter 2

doctrine of God. You must *see* Him and worship Him rightly, or you cannot do what you're called to do with respect to a person who thinks too highly of him or herself.

God probably won't give you a ministry equal in difficulty to Isaiah's, but He has called you to minister to people who won't always love you for it, especially if you must serve a demigod. If you choose to be faithful, humble, and courageous, He will reward you richly even if, by all earthly appearances, nothing changes. Sometimes, though, difficult people do change after many years of faithful ministry have been poured out on them, and in those cases, the rewards come in this age as well as the age to come.

It's hard to minister to difficult people, but in some ways it's actually harder not to. The path of least resistance often leads to a noisy soul in you *as well as* in the one you're not helping, and it leads to the avoided problem growing progressively worse. Think about it. Remember Proverbs 28:1? Cowardice and wickedness go hand in hand, as do righteousness and courage. The fruit of the Spirit is with the faithful ones. Would you rather have a problem-free life with a noisy soul, or a life wrought with problems but blessed by the grace of God? What would you be like in a year if, between now and then, you consistently chose faithfulness over safety, one decision at a time?

Sometimes the best way to love and serve someone is to refrain from giving them what they want. Manipulative folks can be like a spoiled toddler repeatedly throwing his toy on the floor, expecting his parent to pick it up again. The first time the parent doesn't comply, the child will arch his back in a rage. The absolute worst thing you could do for him would be to give him what he wants.

If one person in a contentious relationship pursues humility and repentance and the other one does not, there necessarily is a division between the two people. If the biblically thinking and acting person leaves the relationship, they often will be accused of bringing division, when it's actually the other person's sin that is the source of the rift. The responsibility for repairing the broken relationship belongs to the offending person, and nothing but repentance can accomplish that repair. If the sinned-against person, out of misguided kindness, chooses to maintain false peace, they can be guilty of perpetuating an environment that calls evil good and good evil. Lovingly removing yourself from a relationship can't stop the other person from lying to himself, but at least you will not be aiding and abetting him in his lies.

If you are seeking to interrupt a pattern of abuse and dysfunction in your family, you're doing something radical. It's not going to be easy. If your mom, for instance, is a control freak, she may want more influence than she should have in your life. You do have to honor her, but honoring her doesn't mean giving her everything she wants, including unfettered access to your family.

In fact, one of the best ways you can honor your mom, even though she may never see it as honoring, is to do everything you can to stop the effects of her sin from passing on to her kids and grandkids. Include her in your life if you possibly can, but you and your spouse must set the ground rules for her interaction with you all—she cannot be allowed to control the parameters of your relationship. The two of you have the privilege of doing the very important work of modeling for your children how to love, care for, and refuse to be controlled by difficult people as you serve your mom.

Caveat: The culture tells us we need to remove all the haters and all the toxic people from our lives. I do want you to keep in mind that the Bible does not teach this. God often sends us difficult people we cannot get away from in order to mature us in our love for Him and others, and to help us die to ourselves. God is good and He does good, and if He gives you a difficult person, He has done so for your good.

Having said that, though, keep in mind that Jesus Himself did not allow His own mother to have control over Him.

While he was still speaking to the people, behold, his mother and his brothers stood outside, asking to speak to him. But he replied to the man who told him, "Who is my mother, and who are my brothers?" And stretching out his hand toward his disciples, he said, "Here are my mother and my brothers! For whoever does the will of my Father in heaven is my brother and sister and mother."

Matthew 12:46–50

But He did care for her and see to her needs, particularly as her oldest believing Son:

When Jesus saw his mother and the disciple whom he loved standing nearby, he said to his mother, "Woman, behold, your son!" Then he said to the disciple, "Behold, your mother!" And from that hour the disciple took her to his own home.

John 19:26–27

We know Jesus loved Mary because He is love incarnate, but His mission in life was to do the will of the Father, and He didn't allow even His mother to interfere with that. The people who got the most and best of His time were the ones who also did the will of the Father. It would not have been loving toward Mary or faithful to her soul if Jesus would have given her even one inch of the Father's place in His life. It's a bit shocking that Jesus did not even go out to speak to Mary the day she attempted to call Him away from the people He was teaching, but I'm thankful He gave us the opportunity to think deeply about the ways biblical love sometimes manifests itself in our lives.

Remember divine simplicity: wisdom and love are the same thing. Godly wisdom is loving, and godly love is wise. Wisdom is willing to endure the anger of a child, or of an old lady, or of a selfish spouse in order to help them see themselves clearly and grow. You can wrongly choose to have a vindictive motive as you withdraw from someone, which will not draw God's favor. Keep that in mind. It is possible, though, to withdraw lovingly from people. If you learn your own soul noise tells (having trouble sleeping when you normally do not, compulsive eating, clenching your jaw, repeating a conversation over and over in your head, insert your own here), Lord willing, you will repent of your unloving attitudes more quickly and your care for others will be increasingly pure.

One of the most difficult things about putting distance between yourself and a manipulative person, or keeping your kids from a selfish grandparent, is that they likely will accuse you of being unforgiving and unkind. They may do so pitifully, with eyes full of very convincing tears that cause others to see you as the villain as well. You absolutely must stick to your guns, trusting Christ with your reputation. Answer questions graciously when you must answer them, and understand that you don't owe an explanation to everyone who asks. Do not, under any circumstances, give yourself permission to return evil for evil. You will fail at this, no doubt, and need forgiveness from God and others, over and over again.

You may experience false guilt when you choose to distance yourself from someone, meaning that you might feel badly when you haven't actually sinned. Work through any genuine guilt you have with the Lord, but don't accept any unbiblical burdens on your conscience, whether from your own thoughts or someone else's. Further, it's important to understand that love is patient, kind, and unselfish, but it doesn't necessarily follow that you will miss your difficult person when they are not with you. You likely don't always have warm feelings for them, but biblical love often exists independently of feelings. Their presence is not a joy, and in those cases, you have the privilege of loving them by choice, freely of yourself and for God's sake, not because they are intrinsically worthy of love or fun to be around. You may well have to fight to love them, going to the Lord for forgiveness for your heart attitudes many times per day during some seasons. Don't give up.

Notice the three faces on the godlike person in our diagram. Difficult people can and do change their demeanors, sometimes as a reaction and sometimes deliberately when it suits them to do so. If crying, even asking for forgiveness without turning from sin, has worked to get them their way in the past, they will do that. If smiling and being extra nice previously helped them to regain control over their little worlds, they will readily employ that method as well. You may have tried this yourself. Have you ever said, "I tried being nice and he still won't change!"? Be steadfast and immovable, reflecting Christ for His sake, regardless of the outcome. And recognize that sometimes people's repentance is not genuine, but rather is coercive in nature.

When a person does start being kind for coercive reasons, it can put you in a tough position. First of all, you can't infallibly know what their reasons are. Demigod-like people do sometimes change; it usually takes years if it happens at all, but you don't want to discount the possibility out of hand. Still, if they have lied to you repeatedly in the past, it would be wise to guard your heart against getting your hopes up too much. You must forgive them repeatedly when asked, but that does not mean you owe the person your trust. If a person were caught stealing multiple times, you'd be a fool (and unloving) to put them in charge of the church treasury. Extending forgiveness to a sexual abuser does not mean that they get access to their victim again, or possibly to other potential victims, especially if their sin has been against children. If the person is humble and truly repentant, loving God and loving others, they would never dare ask any such thing. They would faithfully accept the consequences and fallout of their own sin on themselves, difficult as it no doubt would be. If a person becomes sullen about others' lack of trust in them, they are inwardly focused and absolutely not to be trusted. Do not be a coward in this. Be kind, but firm.

You can and should walk other people through their ungracious attitudes toward the possibly repentant person, but be willing to listen to their concerns as well. They may be seeing something you're blind to. Again, cynicism is unloving, but so is foolishness. Wise as serpents *and* innocent as doves (Matthew 10:16) – there is no contradiction there. Help one another make much of Christ in your lives.

Withholding your trust and full fellowship from someone who has demonstrated a long-standing pattern of deception and selfishness does not have to stem from a bitter or unforgiving heart. It might, and you must keep a well-functioning conscience in order to conduct yourself in a godly manner. As you navigate all of this, the best-case scenario is for you to ask some good, wise, sturdy friends who know you well and have a history of lovingly confronting you for help in bringing clarity and sanity to your thoughts. Ministering to difficult people can make you feel crazy at times, and it can powerfully tempt you to sin.

Bring a sturdy friend with you as often as possible when you need to confront or have a difficult conversation with a coercive person. Ideally, they can help you honor the Lord in what you say and do, and also be a witness to any mental manipulation that takes place. If you have been manipulated frequently in your life, you may succumb to it more easily than you realize and your friend can help you tell the difference between what is real and what isn't. If your friend isn't used to the dynamics of coercion, you may have to help them see clearly as well. Communicate as clearly and humbly as you can what they might be missing, and be willing to listen to their feedback in return. In general, men are better at this than women are. In general.

In an environment characterized by manipulation, as when a demigod works all things for his glory, any person who is humble and begins to try to speak into the situation becomes a scapegoat. If you recall from the Old Testament, the sins of the people were symbolically placed on the head of a goat, and then the goat was driven outside of the camp. Scapegoats are also a key part of the worship structure in a demigod-centered scenario.

Often, this is accomplished by accusing the would-be helper of being self-righteous and unforgiving, like I mentioned earlier. Sometimes the helper actually is sinning in her responses, and it's true to say that no person's motives are ever fully pure. Often, though, the concern being voiced is offered with fear, prayer, love, and faithfulness, with the confronting person risking further sin against herself to play a part in what she hopes will be a redemptive solution. If she is a "the log is in my eye" kind of person, she may, in good faith, take responsibility for the speck of impurity in her own motives, which unwittingly plays into the demigod's hands as he shifts the focus off himself and punishes her instead. In a sense, everyone involved is moved to call evil good and good evil. In the worst cases, this pattern repeats itself *ad infinitum* and no real change ever occurs.

If you are called to serve someone in this situation you will have to walk in the Spirit, resembling God in His impassibility, if you are genuinely to be helpful. Let's say a man you know is married to a woman who demands worship, and he has been motivated by a desire to live with her in an understanding way, but his kindness doesn't lead her to repentance. She only becomes more and more entitled and selfish. He is frazzled and exasperated, which the wife interprets as grievous sin against herself, so she assumes a victim role and continues to punish him, rather than taking responsibility for herself. An unwise counselor could further complicate the situation by emphasizing the very true idea that no problem is ever entirely one person's fault. Again, this is true, but the wife will leverage it to her own advantage, finally feeling understood. She will say that, yes, she knows she's difficult, but her husband thinks he's perfect and that's hard to live with as well. The sympathetic counselor could end up being putty in her hands in this case.

Each of these folks is controlled by the emotions of the other to some degree. Your best chance at helping them comes through being calm and objective, seeing ways each of them can grow, and understanding that the best thing for one of them is the best thing for both of them. It's not good for the husband just to allow his wife to go on the way she is without leading her toward godliness as best he can, and it's not good for the wife, either. Her soul's blessedness is dependent upon her repentance, and so he must serve her, even though it will be a thankless job and will take a long time to do it. You should both acknowledge the difficulty of his life *and* help him have the God-empowered courage to be faithful to her, even though his life will get harder in the short term. You would be wise to correct him outside his wife's hearing for the most part, because she can't steward any discussion about his faults in a way that will honor God and bless her husband.

He's in a tough spot, which you should acknowledge freely. It's hard to change, but it's harder to stay the same. Avoiding his responsibility by choosing the easy way now will bring a costlier payday down the road in the form of his wife being even more blind, even more selfish and difficult in the future. If he chooses to love her through persistent, consistent correction, the Lord will bless him with patience, joy, and perseverance through the process. If he wants an easier life more than he wants the gifts God has for him, he'll make the wrong choices and get neither.

He will have to examine his own heart and life, repenting for all genuine sin as he becomes aware of it, and he will have to reject the role of scapegoat, refusing to seek forgiveness unless he genuinely has sinned. He cannot allow his wife to use her microscope and scalpel on him in order to avoid taking full responsibility for herself. To well-meaning but naïve onlookers, this will appear prideful at times. They can't know what they don't know, and the man must be controlled by what is best for himself and his wife, regardless of what people think, maintaining a gracious attitude toward everyone involved. You, as his friend, will have to help him keep his focus on the *a se,* simple, impassible, omni-everything-good Lord of the universe, or he has no hope of success. Each of you must be in constant prayer for eyes to see, ears to hear, and hearts that understand, for yourselves and for the unchanging, too-big person. If your friend does this with increasing fidelity, he will have a quiet soul—the blessing of going through a trial with God instead of in opposition to Him. The peace that passes understanding.

No one would willingly choose this path, but the Lord in His kindness often ordains that we can't avoid it. He is good, and what He does is good. Believe that He is, that He rewards those who diligently seek Him, and walk on. In part two of this book, I will lay out some case studies dealing with various iterations of the type of person I have been talking about. This book in no way represents an exhaustive treatment on the subject, but with careful consideration, you will be able to extrapolate from the information I provide and apply it to a wide variety of relational difficulties.

4

The Connection Between Courage and Wisdom

Don't you draw the queen of diamonds, boy; she'll beat you if she's able.

You know the queen of hearts is always your best bet.

Now, it seems to me some fine things have been laid upon your table, but you only want the ones you can't get.

The Eagles

It's easier to take a bullet for someone than it is to die daily for them. It's easier to stand on a corner and herald the gospel to heckling strangers you'll never see again than it is to call a beloved friend or family member to repentance. It's easier to take a month off in order to build wells or houses for impoverished people than it is to fully commit to telling yourself nothing but the truth. All of these things are good to do, but if you never set your face toward doing the second things in each couplet, may I suggest to you that you could be self-deceived? The folks around you will probably will malign you and misunderstand you if you commit to telling the truth to yourself and to them. On the other hand, they will clap for you if you do the seemingly heroic things, and their applause may well contribute to your self-deception—causing you to think more highly of yourself than you ought--when in truth you could be both a coward and a fool.

Here's a question for you: if you were a fool—which I'm not saying you are, but if you were—would you want to know? If you had spiritual egg on your face, would you want someone to tell you or would you want to live on in ignorance? Is it ok with you if people see it, just as long as they pretend that they don't? What does God want you to do about your sin? Are you playing defense attorney for the thing that's trying to kill you?

Imagine that you are walking through the woods and you come upon a raccoon with its leg caught in a trap. If you're not an animal lover, you may have to use your imagination here. Let's say that you are moved with compassion for the adorable, suffering creature and you want to help, but every time you try to reach around the raccoon to free its leg, it thinks you are attacking it and tries to kill you in return! One valid option open to you at that point would be simply to move on and let it die of blood loss or gangrene. If you really care, though, and you're determined to help, you will choose not to take the creature's anger personally, put on a full-arm leather glove, and do what you can to free it and tend to its wounds.

It would be a good exercise to think through that scenario a few times, once with yourself in the role of the raccoon and another with yourself in the role of the rescuer. First, the raccoon. In what scenarios do you resist help you desperately need? Why do you resist? Based on your actions, what is the most important thing to you? If you were honest with yourself, what would you say is the best set of biblical descriptors for your character: wise and courageous, or foolish and cowardly? Will you ask God to help you grow, and seek godly help? The raccoon is foolish; he wants to feel better, but he doesn't realize that, as Jordan Peterson says, what he wants the most is found where he least wants to look for it. How about you, Friend?

Secondly, consider yourself as the wilderness hiker. The would-be helper, if he's wise, compassionate, and courageous, knows that waiting and observing indefinitely won't result in the raccoon's desperate problem being solved. Now, you don't have a moral obligation before God to go around saving raccoons, necessarily, but you absolutely are obligated to serve your brother or sister caught in sin.

One way in which the raccoon metaphor breaks down is that you can make the raccoon receptive to help, with a tranquilizer dart employed to subdue his vigor so you can set his little leg. People are different, obviously, and you are not called to make anyone change. Some ways you can tell you're trying to control their change are when you become angry with them easily, or when you're tempted to despair about their state. The human equivalent of our raccoon is foolish in trying to achieve his goal of feeling better, and the helper can similarly be foolish, either in neglecting his responsibility altogether, or in trying to force help and change on a resistant person.

Sometimes, upon further examination, it's a cobra and not a raccoon in the trap (my eyesight isn't all that great at times), and the best course is to leave it where it is and see to your own safety. You're not required to serve every caught raccoon, or every cobra, but there are people in your sphere of influence that God wants you to glove up and help. If you're reading this, I assume you want to honor God and love people well. That's what He wants for you, too. Are you prepared for the reality that what you want may be where you least want to look for it?

The raccoon most certainly will think you're evil, and well-meaning but foolish bystanders will think you're cruel at times as you afflict even more pain on an already suffering creature. Will you determine to be ok with that? It's a road that no one wants, but all of the best things are at the end of it. Healthy souls, church unity, godly families, and general usefulness to God and His people come through doing the hard but necessary work of biblical wound care.

I've had lots of raccoons in my life, but for years when I would use the trap illustration, I had one particular beloved friend in mind. She was trapped in her own sin, blind, angry, resistant to care, and protected by sincere but misguided and unwise loved ones from the help she needed. She was a too-big person, but almost no one had the insight to view her that way, so they couldn't be of any genuine help (I wasn't the only one truly helping her, but by far most of the folks around her were only aiding her self-deception). By God's grace, she's now out of the trap, and all of the heartache that went into caring for her was worth it many times over. Many of the caught folks I have sought to serve have not changed, but some have. And through the work involved, God has granted me more of the creaturely form—the analogical image—of His aseity and impassibility, for which I have begged Him for years.

Most Christians are not willing to engage in the kind of soul care for which I'm advocating, which is understandable on one level, but it's also foolish and cowardly to avoid it. The problems you ignore almost always get worse with time, and God will make you deal down the line with the gargantuan, mutant, festering form of the thing that would have been much more manageable if you had applied the healing salve earlier.

Often, people see problems somewhat clearly and want to critique them but don't want the relational difficulty that comes with addressing what they see. Instead, they engage in mental and moral gymnastics—an elaborate form of self-deception—to convince themselves they have no responsibility. This is utterly foolish because not only does the other person not get the help they desperately need, but the person doing the justifying has begun to become habituated in lying. They are without truth in their inward parts, which has a domino effect leading to other and increasingly serious cancers of the soul. Eventually, they hold a form (appearance) of godliness, while denying the power thereof. These folks have a spiritual dullness that keeps them from perceiving the danger they're in, and they're vehemently opposed to receiving correction. This is the opposite of humility and godliness. Astoundingly, they beheld a too-big person, and rather than conforming themselves to the image of the true God and calling the other person to the same, the beholder became what they beheld, namely the difficult person who ultimately controlled their behavior, resulting in their conformity to wickedness instead of godliness.

Even though they started out with some measure of a clear view of the false goddess, they will often go so far as to defend the sinning person if another tries to help her. Thus, they are aligned, not with the great God of peace, joy, and freedom, but with the enemy of our souls. It's hard to help, but it's harder not to. Choose your hard wisely.

How about you, friend? Do you strive to tell yourself and others the truth? Do you run toward or away from the people who can help you see yourself clearly? Put another way, do you serve God or Satan? If you really are serving Satan, are you willing to be honest with yourself about that fact? What will happen to you if you continue to deceive yourself?

The too-big person is a liar, and God has given him over to his lies so that he truly believes them, to an extent. His conscience won't be quiet, though, so he's riddled with soul noise. That's why he's so defensive (Proverbs 28:1), why he continually bites the hand that's trying to help him.

There are probably many, many people in your life who are as I have described. You may not recognize all of them because, like I've said, they are inherently deceptive, some of them skillfully so. Part of their deception can be a projection of winsomeness and charm that fools most people; indeed, they may have only a few targets who see the full truth of who they are.

They count on people being cowardly and blind in order for them to maintain control over their facades, and most people are more than willing to comply. Many families do devotions together, are involved in churches, and do copious good deeds, but inwardly are full of deception. Many churches, even churches who have excellent teaching from the pulpit, are filled with people who put on a mask and aren't honest with themselves or anyone else. They rail against the sin that is "out there," and have all the right opinions, all the while being unaware of their own spiritual peril. Even if someone sees through what is going on in these scenarios, the task of speaking up about it is daunting because they know it would earn them nothing but persecution most of the time, at least in the short term.

But what does God want you to do? Are you going to be part of the healthy immune system of the Body, of your family? If you are convicted to begin helping, start small, and definitely start with yourself, because Spirit-wrought self-mastery is the most basic unit of leadership. Doing so will earn you more light, more wisdom from God. You can't export what you don't have yourself. As your eyes are opened to the deception around you it will seem overwhelming, and indeed it is. God hasn't called you to change your whole church today, Friend. Again, start with yourself and with someone you love who is caught, and do the next right thing. Don't heap all of the correction a person needs to hear on them at once, because no one can handle that. God deals with us incrementally but persistently and patiently; you do the same. Honor God and love His people, in spirit and in truth. Beg God for eyes to see, ears to hear, and a heart that understands, and don't ever stop begging. Be a threat to the kingdom of darkness as long as the LORD gives you breath. What's the point of living if not for that?

The ironic truth is that all of the things you're trying to protect, the things that are keeping you from being a wise and courageous truth teller, will elude you if you don't have truth in your inward parts. What you want can be found, but it's only to be discovered on the path you might fear to tread. If God does grant your desires to you the easy way, they will bring you misery. Camp out on the following questions before you continue reading. It would be good for you to write over your answers and meditate on them before the Lord, inviting Him to open your eyes and lead you in all wisdom and insight. Remember that forgiveness, joy, and freedom are yours for the asking, but you have to ask (1 John 1:9).

Do you ever pray to get sick so that you can avoid a difficult task you're called to do? As the time draws near, are you tempted to exaggerate an ailment so you can stay home?

Do you ever blame your sinful anger on someone who sins against you, or on being hungry or tired, or on a difficult season of life? What effect is this having on your soul?

Do you keep your word, even when it's inconvenient to you to do so? Do you show up to things on time, when you said you would be there?

How do you react when someone points out a sin or shortcoming in you? Their approach shouldn't matter if you love the truth and want to honor God. Your reaction will reveal what you want the most. Again, the choice is between foolishness and wisdom, cowardice and courage.

Have you ever been accused of excusing things in yourself that you hate in other people? Is there any truth to the accusation?

Do you ever experience persecution? Why or why not? Are you ok with being misunderstood if you know you're doing the right thing? Do you think it's possible that you mistake biblical love for persecution? Are you willing to ask a person who loves you and isn't afraid to wound you to help you answer these questions?

Can you think of any other areas in which you are not truthful with yourself? How will you respond to that knowledge? Do you understand that moving on without dealing with your lies is indeed a choice, and that it has serious consequences?

Remember that the righteous is as bold as a lion. When you have truth in your inward parts, you will have a quiet soul and more of the courage you need to minister to difficult people without being overcome. Learn to identify your "tells" so you know when to examine your heart. If I can't sleep well, if I'm clenching my jaw, or if I'm tempted to escape from life through overeating or through binge reading novels, there's a good chance my conscience is trying to get my attention. Your revealing traits will probably be different than mine and it would be good for you to finely tune your perception of them.

Intense soul care ministry will provide the heat to your life that causes your spiritual impurities to rise to the top. The blessing of this is that once you see something, you can confess it and repent for it! Difficult people can't cause your sin; they can only help to draw out what already lives in your heart. Tell yourself the truth, tell God the truth, ask for and accept His forgiveness, and get back in there. Your failures will move you toward dependence upon God and greater steadfastness if you respond rightly to them. Take a bullet for your friends if it comes to that, but what they need more is the truth. Will you commit to being the best friend you can be, starting now?

5

King Saul

All I can hear
I me mine, I me mine, I me mine
Even those tears
I me mine, I me mine, I me mine

No one's frightened of playing it
Everyone's saying it
Flowing more freely than wine

All through the day
I me mine

The Beatles

As I was writing this book, my pastor was teaching our church through 1 Samuel and he shared some profound insights into the character of King Saul as he was doing so. Bryan was called to another church before he could finish the book, but his teaching caused me to dig into the text myself and to study Saul and David's dynamic because the connection between them and what I'm trying to communicate here was undeniable. What follows is a blend of Pastor Bryan Ragsdale's[5] thoughts and my own; I am, of course, deeply indebted to him for the content of this chapter.

One of the key themes of the book of 1 Samuel is that, while man looks on the outward appearance, God looks at the heart (1 Samuel 16:7). Most people, even in the church, never do learn to see more deeply than outward appearance and natural gifting, into the character of a man (have you ever seen a church neglect God's wisdom about looking to a man's leadership at home to determine whether or not he can be an officer in the church?). In God's kindness, He used Israel's wickedly longed-for king to show David how to look beyond what lies on the surface, which would serve the man after God's own heart well as the means of granting him the wisdom he would need to lead God's people himself one day. Naivete is not befitting a good

---

[5] https://www.grace-bc.com/tag/1st-samuel/

king, and the Lord delivered David from his through suffering and persecution.

Israel was jealous of the other nations and wanted a king like they had, so YHWH gave them one. In many ways, Saul looked to be everything one could want: he was tall, extraordinarily handsome, from a wealthy family, and unlike anyone else in their midst. The people received him joyfully.

As an aside, it's worth noting that every person alive, without exception, is tempted to think more of himself than he ought to think. It's exponentially harder for someone to have sober judgment when he is gifted by the LORD with looks, intelligence, money, talent, etc., and when the people around him sing his praises. Do you have eyes to see through someone's giftings to their character? What characteristics might you look for if you want to know who someone really is? Do you ignore your own sin patterns and weaknesses, emphasizing your gifting instead? How would you know if you were doing so? Do you justify sins or shortcomings in yourself that you hate and condemn in others?

Even though Saul ran from leadership at first (1 Samuel 10:21-22), you can see throughout the book that he eventually felt entitled to his position and demanded loyalty and service from others. Incidentally, this devolution may well result when you lay hands on someone hastily—if a person is not qualified and you give him a leadership position, you're saying something God has not said about him (1 Corinthians 12:28), and you're contributing to his self-deception, which will spiral out of control if he has a longing for power or position sans the requisite character. The implications could not be more serious, and the effects on the church are catastrophic. The church as a whole will believe what you have implicitly said about the unqualified man, which will cause them to think wrongly about the Lord, His plan for His church, and even for themselves as they imitate what they should not—namely, the example wrongly held up for them. They will become what they behold, for ruin rather than for restoration, and the leaders who installed these men will bear the responsibility before the LORD.

The same is true if you marry someone whose passion is not to make much of God. Do you want a king like all the other nations, or rather, do you want to be married like all the other ladies (or guys)? What would happen if the LORD heard and answered your cries? Would the result be ruin for you, or restoration? If restoration, how difficult would the path need to be in your case to bring you to it? The consequences will be exactly what you need to produce the wisdom you lack, provided you commit your path to the Lord during the process. Not everyone does this, of course.

And in that day you will cry out because of your king, whom you have chosen for yourselves, but the LORD will not answer you in that day.

1 Samuel 8:18

Saul was not a leader. He passively hid among the baggage when Samuel called for him, he superstitiously and illegitimately sacrificed to YHWH and blamed Samuel for it (1 Samuel 13:9-12), he took credit for his son's victory in battle, and he only partially obeyed the Lord in the battle with the Amalekites (chapter 15), all the while claiming righteousness (vv. 19-21) and feeling entitled to Samuel's praise as he blamed the people for his own sin and disobedience. I have by no means given an exhaustive list of Saul's moral failures to this point, but this should suffice to show who Saul was before he ever met David. Nothing that follows should surprise anyone given what we know to be true about Saul thus far. We don't have to assume Saul's motives because we see them clearly: he is motivated by self-interest and self-glory.

In 1 Samuel 8:11 and following, the people of Israel were warned that their king would be a taker, and he was. They rejected YHWH as king and got exactly what they wanted, to their own ruin and detriment. Rather than honoring the Lord in light of Samuel's dire warnings, which would have resulted in blessing for Saul and for the nation, Saul proceeded in his religious hypocrisy and selfishness. Thus YHWH and Saul rejected one another's kingship. The kingdom of God is always an assault on the kingdom of this world, the kingdom of darkness, and as such it is always satanically persecuted. I'll speak more on that assertion later as we discuss the relationship between Saul and David, who was a type or a foreshadowing of Christ Himself.

When Samuel rebuked Saul in 1 Samuel 15:19 and 22-24, the people sacrificed to the LORD. Pastor Bryan said that, given their lack of actual repentance, it was as if they bought the impassible God flowers in order to smooth things over. Saul did admit he had sinned... but he blamed the people for it. Then he appealed to Samuel for things to go back to the way they were (v. 30) and for Samuel to honor him before the people.

Unbelievable. But if you know (or are) a too-big person, you know that tactics like these are standard operating procedure. They want all of the relational blessings that faithfulness produces without actually having to be faithful, and they feel confused and victimized when they don't get them.

As the Lord rejects the people's king, the king according to outward appearance, we come to the king that the Lord Himself chooses irrespective of man's appraisal. Immediately after Samuel anoints David as king, following the Lord's directive, we read something peculiar: "Now the Spirit of the LORD departed from Saul, and a harmful spirit from the LORD tormented him." 1 Samuel 16:14.

Saul is not unique by any means; in fact, people like him are quite common. I am positing that there is a reason why people like Saul seem to operate by a common playbook. Even though they are not all exactly the same, the commonality is unmistakable, and they don't seem to need a human teacher in order to learn the same wicked tactics that have always been shared by this particular type of manipulative person. This passage from James corroborates this hypothesis:

Who is wise and understanding among you? By his good conduct let him show his works in the meekness of wisdom. But if you have bitter jealousy and selfish ambition in your hearts, do not boast and be false to the truth. This is not the wisdom that comes down from above, but is earthly, unspiritual, ***demonic****. For where jealousy and selfish ambition exist, there will be disorder and every vile practice. But the wisdom from above is first pure, then peaceable, gentle, open to reason, full of mercy and good fruits, impartial and sincere. And a harvest of righteousness is sown in peace by those who make peace.*

James 3:13–18

It is often impossible to tell with folks like Saul whether or not they are saved, and it can be a fruitless occupation to try to determine their status before the LORD with any kind of certainty. In a few verses after the passage above, James tells us to resist the devil and he will flee from us. Satan's goal, of course, is to keep people from getting saved, but if he can't do that, he wants us to be as ineffective as possible. A believer can't be demon-possessed, that's true, but most *un*believers are under demonic influence without being possessed either. Satan's greatest weapon is falsehood, and Christians lie to themselves with great frequency and creativity just like unbelievers do. Our enemy knows we are carried away and enticed by the desires of our hearts, and he studies us to know what those desires are. All he has to do is dangle the carrot most of the time and off we go to do his will. It's not that difficult, really. If you don't resist him, believer, he won't flee from you. If you don't resist him, unbeliever, he won't flee from you.

As David enters the scene in 1 Samuel 16, he is not privy to what Saul has previously done as far as we know. David is brought to Saul, and the music David plays allays Saul's demonic suffering, at least for a time. At this point, presumably, Saul still has the will and ability to resist the devil, and David's presence and ministry strengthen him to do so. As a result, we are told that Saul loved David greatly. This love, though, was not love characterized by the fruit of the Spirit, as such love is moved to esteem and encourage the best in the other. He loved David because David's ministry benefitted him. Saul's "love" became jealous and suspicious (1 Samuel 18:9) when David began to receive more praise than Saul. When this happened, Saul began to throw spears at David when David played for him. He no longer resisted the devil, and so the devil no longer fled. David prospered because the Lord was with him, and Saul went from bad to worse because the Lord was in opposition to him (James 4:6). These two men were on a collision course for conflict, even though David did everything he could to be at peace with Saul. The enemy hates godly people, and he attacks them through people who are susceptible to his wiles, as Saul was and as all people who think too highly of themselves are.

Even though Saul was now actively trying to kill David, when Saul sent David into a battle against the Philistines in order to bring about his death, promising the hand of his daughter as a reward for victory, David was humble and grateful at the prospect of being the king's son-in-law. He put the best construction on Saul's behavior, taking him at face value. This is the inclination of a humble, gracious, forgiving man.

David won the battle, but Saul gave his daughter to someone else. He gave David his other daughter, Michal, instead, specifically saying in private that he intended her to be a snare to him. David overlooked the sleight and accepted Michal with characteristic gratitude. At this point, David was longsuffering and not easily offended. It may be said that he should have been catching on by now, but honest people default to trust, and David was honest. As you consider his future failures, keep in mind that his humility is the best predictor of David's future spiritual success in response to his failure, even as Saul's cowardice, passivity, and deception are the predictors of Saul's future downfall.

As David slew the Philistines to win his bride and to honor his king, and Saul saw that the LORD was with David, 1 Samuel 18:29 says that Saul was even more afraid of David, and thus was David's enemy continually. David did Saul nothing but good (1 Samuel 19:4), but Saul was afraid of David. Why? If you're recalling our earlier discussion about the conscience, you are probably remembering what happens when someone's conscience is condemning them: they run when no one is chasing them. Saul has fear where there is no external perceived threat, and we are told explicitly that he has sinful anger and jealousy toward David. Peace and confidence are not compatible with rebellion against God and hatred of people, and so Saul has soul noise. So it is for all too-big people.

*And **Saul was very angry**, and this saying displeased him. He said, "They have ascribed to David ten thousands, and to me they have ascribed thousands, and what more can he* *have but the kingdom?" And Saul eyed David from that day on.*

The next day ***a harmful spirit from God rushed upon Saul****, and he raved within his house while David was playing the lyre, as he did day by day. Saul had his spear in his hand. And Saul hurled the spear, for he thought, "I will pin David to the wall." But David evaded him twice.*

Saul was afraid of David ***because the LORD was with him*** *but had departed from Saul. So Saul removed him from his presence and made him a commander of a thousand. And he went out and came in before the people. And David had success in all his undertakings, for the LORD was with him. And when Saul saw that he had great success, he stood in fearful awe of him.*

1 Samuel 18:8-15

But when Saul saw and knew that the LORD was with David, and that Michal, Saul's daughter, loved him, Saul was even more afraid of David. So ***Saul was David's enemy continually****.*

1 Samuel 18:28–29

The text directly tells us there is a literal demonic influence here, but if you were only observing the situation without the Bible's commentary on it, James 3 (above) gives ample exposition of the source of this type of behavior. James gives you behind-the-scenes information.

If two people came to you for help with conflict resolution, presenting similarly to this text, would you mutualize the blame? Do your presuppositions require you to do so? What would your reasoning be, assuming you would approach the situation in this way? The more the LORD was with David, the less Saul operated in good faith toward David. It is always the case that the person who feels entitled to receive worship both admires and wants to eradicate others who excel. This is due to the demonic nature of jealousy. If a person loves the Lord, they will rejoice when God gets glory, even if it isn't from them. They will love the people who resemble Jesus the most. If you hate (are jealous of) godly people, you hate their God. It's not complicated.

In the verses that follow these, you can see malice, cowardice, lying, and passivity (v. 17, 19, 21-25) in Saul toward David, which is in line with "every vile thing" from James.

Again, consider Saul's fear of David. What is the reason for his fear? If you didn't know these men and they came to you for help, would you be able to counsel Saul through his fear, or would you be tempted to blame Saul's reaction on David's demeanor in some way?

Is the conflict between Saul and David like or unlike the conflict between Euodia and Syntyche in Philippians 4? How do you know? Hypothetically, how do you think Paul would have framed his instructions to David and Saul, if he had had an opportunity to speak to them?

Saul distrusted David *for no good reason,* and soon after, David began to distrust Saul in return, but with a different cause for his distrust: Saul was untrustworthy and David was not a fool. David's distrust of Saul was sane. In response to Jonathan's rebuke, Saul swore to Jonathan he wouldn't kill David (1 Samuel 19:6), and then he promptly threw a spear at him again. There was no culpability in David's lack of trust; he had good reason. When words and actions are contradictory, which should you believe? Is it always a sin (a failure to "hope all things, bear all things, believe all things, endure all things" per 1 Corinthians 13:7) not to take someone at face value, or is it possible that choosing to believe someone's words in the face of contrary evidence serves the purposes of the father of lies more than YHWH's?

Jonathan still believed his father's words and urged David to go back to the palace to eat with the king. What if David had capitulated? How should a persecuted person respond to well-meaning folks who urge them to do things that will put them in harm's way?

When David did not show up to eat, Saul raged at his son, attacking him verbally and physically, and playing the victim (1 Samuel 20:30-33). He did something similar (minus the physical violence) to his daughter Michal, David's wife, when she helped her husband escape his murderous plot (1 Samuel 19:17). Saul was the sinner, but he put the blame on those who thwarted his sin, calling evil good and good evil, denying reality. Sometimes this is called gaslighting, and it's also part of the enemy's tired, worn, yet oddly effective playbook. Good men and women, by the way, never have a victim mentality. Humility and gratitude are antithetical to feeling slighted by God and others.

You see more of Saul playing the victim, being paranoid (running when not being chased), manipulating, and engaging in self-pity in 1 Samuel 22:7-8, and also in verse 13. Many people capitulated to him and aided his sin. People like Saul, whether male or female, find no lack of sycophants, cowards, and weak people to do their bidding. Even Jonathan did so to a degree, with no ill motive, but he deferred to David's judgment after all. When Ahimelech defended his own innocence as well as David's, Saul had his lackeys put him and the priests to death. It's becoming easier all the time, in the course of our discussion here, to see why one should identify and deal with jealousy and selfish ambition in their infancy, and also not to promote leaders who are characterized by these things. Those traits are hard to battle, but it's harder in the long run when you don't deal with them. Jesus calls sinful anger murder for good reason. Be killing sin, as John Owen said, or it will be killing you. And those around you, to boot.

Saul continued his petty, relentless, murderous pursuit of David. The text indicates that Saul knew the Lord was with David, and yet he opposed him, meaning that he explicitly opposed YHWH as well. He rightly esteemed David and valued him, but he simultaneously violently and jealously fixated on him. Demigod-like, too-big people often do have an unrelenting perseverance as they harass their targets. A normal person would move on with their lives and get a new hobby, but not these folks. Perseverance—good, true perseverance—is Spirit-wrought, and it seems that this kind of perverted perseverance is supernatural in origin as well.

The question for the observer and the would-be helper is always one of how much accountability and responsibility should be put on the demigod. He genuinely seems to be unaware of his own inconsistency and so the impulse of the gracious, truthful folks around him is to give him "grace," and not to be too tough on him because of his seemingly low capacity. You would not penalize an average person for not being able to throw a hundred mile an hour fastball, right? However, the argument from Romans 1-2 is that every person without exception is without excuse when it comes to their obedience to God, and that is especially true for the Jew or the Christian: You, therefore, who teach another, do you not teach yourself? Saul knew and rejected the truth, and God gave him over to his debased mind, which increased rather than decreased his responsibility before the LORD even though he genuinely was increasingly blind to himself and his own motives. YHWH did not give Saul a pass, and neither did David or Samuel. His blindness was a willful, culpable blindness.

Notice that as David worshipped YHWH in spirit and in truth, the Lord gave David eyes to see, ears to hear, and a heart that understands. "A heart that understands" is one way of saying "wisdom;" the fear of YHWH is the beginning of wisdom, remember? Christ is wisdom incarnate (1 Corinthians 1:24, Proverbs 8) and those who revere Him resemble Him in His wisdom. Saul did not fear the Lord, so he did not have a heart of understanding, which is why he couldn't make decisions for himself. He was dependent upon others for the wisdom he did not have—first Samuel, and then a medium who, although she was an agent of Satan, was wiser than Saul by far. Even as an unbeliever, she had some fear of YHWH, whereas Saul

none. The Lord did not answer Saul when he
ired of Him, and He took Samuel away from Saul
dgment against him, too, since Saul didn't heed
uel's words when he had the opportunity. So what
aul do? He consulted a witch to bring Samuel back
the dead. And so you see that our consideration
aul's kingly life began and ended with his
nitment to no less than Satan, not YHWH, even
gh Saul would likely have been self-deceptively
rant to that fact. Saul increasingly resembled the
he worshipped with blind eyes, deaf ears, and a
heart. When you see those characteristics in
one, they are never spiritually well. Never. Even
one with a low IQ can be profoundly wise if they
hip the LORD in spirit and in truth. Saul
nbled a brute beast as what wisdom he did have,
acterizing true manhood, effaced and then
orated from his life altogether. He did not eat grass
Nebuchadnezzar did, but I would argue that his
al blindness exceeded Nebuchadnezzar's. God

restored Nebuchadnezzar to his right mind, but Saul faced God's wrath of abandonment.

Saul never stopped invoking YHWH's name in all of this. Friends, don't take someone's church attendance, Scripture usage, or "God language" to mean that they love God. What do their actions say? Are they denying by their lives what they know full well to be true, not just because the testimony of God is written on their hearts, but because they have knowledge of the truth through diligent study that hasn't transformed them? Does your level of accountability for them model YHWH's own, or are you aiding them further in their self-deception? This is not a call to be unkind (we will look at David's outstanding modeling of how to love and respond to such a person in the next chapter). Would you counsel Saul by taking it easy on him because he doesn't know any better (bless him wittle heart)? What level of responsibility would you place on David to do better in his relationship with Saul? Do not look on the outward appearance, Friend. It sometimes happen that both people in a difficult relationship ke Saul, even while both initially present as being like David. You will need a heart that rstands in order to see clearly. This book will help but not without the requisite insight that only the t can bring.

key observation you can make that will help you rn the condition of a person's soul is the presence sence of soul noise (see chapter 2). This may well fficult at the outset because a person who is facing tless Satanic persecution will often be unstable. they willing to acknowledge what sinful anger do have, embracing the promise of cleansing, veness, and help from the Lord found in 1 John If they have been suffering for a long time, they need your patience and kindness, and their path not be linear. Are they willing to pursue the other on's best interest, or are they just self-protective, y, and vindictive? If someone is willing to trend in ight direction, humility wise, their soul will begin to calm almost immediately and you will begin to see a reduction in what the world calls "mental health issues," as well as an increase in wisdom, self-insight, and godly sorrow, leading to repentance. The conscience is always the key, and it goes a long way toward exposing someone's self-deception. If they are lying, even if they believe their own lies, or if they are self-righteous, they will not have experiential peace because peace is a facet of love, which is fruit of the Spirit. All of the anxiety issues, including the paranoia we observed in Saul, are related to a noisy soul, a conscience that's not right with God.

In the next chapter, you will see David's example of how to face this kind of evil persecution in a way that leaves you with a quiet soul. Nobody can stop you from loving God and loving others, and as you do those things, the God of peace will be with you.

David was remarkable, even though he was fallen. His life and example point toward Christ, the true and greater David, whose kingdom also drew the lerous hatred of the kingdom of darkness, but st defeated Satan fully and finally, crushing the of the serpent of old by His perfect life, death, rection, and ascension. It does not look like the ıy is defeated right now, but he is. If you are facing ind of persecution I'm describing in this book, you need to remind yourself of this fact over and over ı. "You're not David!", as a famous pastor said. you're not, but if you live faithfully to Christ and ı union with Him, you will fill up what is lacking hrist's afflictions. Satan and his flying monkeys t finished hating Jesus yet, and since you represent resemble Him, their ire falls on you. Both David's Christ's lives show us what satanic oppression s like, and it's not what people often imagine. They show us how to engage that oppression. The last rvation I want to make about Saul's life shows the ıt and climax of his deception, namely being ıl and seemingly repentant. This tactic rather than play of rage is the most sinister lie because it's the convincing one to the good people the enemy most wants to fool and to render ineffective. David's response is masterful and instructive.

By the way, King Ahab was a weak and ineffective leader, too, and his wife was not his Davidic, Christlike counterpart. If you respond poorly to persecution, the enemy gets a two for one. More often than not his playbook serves him very well, which is why he has not edited it in all of these years.

6

The Image of Satan

ase allow me to introduce myself. I'm a man of wealth and taste.

The Rolling Stones

T last observation I wanted to make into the life of S deserves its own chapter because it represents the e stage, terminal cancer of satanic hypocrisy. Will y please read this chapter carefully, with yourself in r l first of all? If you think honestly and soberly a t this chapter, I trust that you will see how easy it c d be to end up where King Saul did, spiritually s king. If for some time you have made pursuing l ness and honesty a serious goal, *this is not describing* y and you are not equally at fault for the conflicts in y contentious relationship. The difficulty, though, is that most folks who are like King Saul think they are the victims in every circumstance. Proceed wisely.

> *Afterward David also arose and went out of the cave, and called after Saul, "My lord the king!" And when Saul looked behind him, David bowed with his face to the earth and paid homage. And David said to Saul, "Why do you listen to the words of men who say, 'Behold, David seeks your harm'? Behold, this day your eyes have seen how the LORD gave you today into my hand in the cave. And some told me to kill you, but I spared you. I said, 'I will not put out my hand against my lord, for he is the LORD's anointed.' See, my father, see the corner of your robe in my hand. For by the fact that I cut off the corner of your robe and did not kill you, you may know and see that there is no wrong or treason in my hands. I have not sinned against you, though you hunt my life to take it. May the LORD judge between me and you, may the LORD avenge me against you, but my hand shall not be against you. As the proverb of the ancients says, 'Out of the wicked comes wickedness.' But my hand shall not be against you. After whom has the king of Israel come out? After whom do you pursue? After a dead dog! After a flea! May the LORD therefore be judge and give sentence between me and you, and see to it and plead my cause and deliver me from your hand."*

As soon as David had finished speaking these words to Saul, Saul said, "Is this your voice, my son David?" And Saul lifted up his voice and wept. He said to David, "You are more righteous than I, for you have repaid me good, whereas I have repaid you evil. And you have declared this day how you have dealt well with me, in that you did not kill me when the LORD put me into your hands. For if a man finds his enemy, will he let him go away safe? So may the LORD reward you with good for what you have done to me this day. And now, behold, I know that you shall surely be king, and that the kingdom of Israel shall be established in your hand. Swear to me therefore by the LORD that you will not cut off my offspring after me, and that you will not destroy my name out of my father's house." And David swore this to Saul. Then Saul went home, but David and his men went up to the stronghold.

1 Samuel 24:8–22

I is passage, David tells the truth about Saul, and i kes YHWH's judgment, seeking only God's glory a Saul's good. You can see here David's outstanding e iple of honoring Saul, while also unflinchingly s king of him the way Scripture does.

Contemplate Saul's words of "repentance": super encouraging, aye? How would you interpret Saul's words, if they were the words of a counselee sitting before you? See 1 Samuel 26:1 and 27:11. A person's past patterns are the best predictors of their futures. Notice that there's no drama in the text, no angst in David about whether or not Saul was repentant. David stayed in exile because he wasn't a fool—he didn't trust Saul.

What would you say to a person who was trying to help David and Saul, who admonished both of them for their lack of trust for one another? Trust is the foundation for any good relationship, after all. Should David have "put the best construction" on Saul's words? Why or why not?

As was his pattern, Saul is masquerading as an angel of light here.

Saul recognized David's voice and said, "Is this your voice, my son David?" And David said, "It is my voice, my lord, O king." And he said, "Why does my lord pursue after his servant? For what have I done? What evil is on my hands?

w therefore let my lord the king hear the words of his ʼant. If it is the LORD who has stirred you up against may he accept an offering, but if it is men, may they be ;ed before the LORD, for they have driven me out this 'ay that I should have no share in the heritage of the RD, saying, 'Go, serve other gods.' Now therefore, let ny blood fall to the earth away from the presence of the RD, for the king of Israel has come out to seek a single a like one who hunts a partridge in the mountains."

Saul said, "I have sinned. Return, my son David, for I no more do you harm, because my life was precious in eyes this day. Behold, I have acted foolishly, and have made a great mistake."

1 Samuel 26:17–21

n Saul said to David, "Blessed be you, my son David! u will do many things and will succeed in them." So)avid went his way, and Saul returned to his place.

1 Samuel 26:25

n David said in his heart, "Now I shall perish one day e hand of Saul. There is nothing better for me than that uld escape to the land of the Philistines. Then Saul will despair of seeking me any longer within the borders of Israel, and I shall escape out of his hand."

1 Samuel 27:1

See how much faith David had in Saul's "repentance?" Would you be tempted to accuse him of being uncharitable in his heart toward Saul? Would it be appropriate to admonish David for not being "in faith for the process?" It's even possible that Saul meant what he said at the time, or thought that he did. Was David at fault for not trusting Saul? Was he failing to trust the Lord?

How would you counsel a humble, submissive wife who was encouraged by words like this from her wicked husband?

It's not popular, not considered gracious, to take someone's actions rather than their words at face value. David's response in our passage is not because he isn't ng room for the grace of God, but because he ly has discerned that sometimes the LORD ctably hardens a person's heart.

needed to be gentle and lowly, and to learn from d, but he persecuted him instead. He understood admired who and what David was—the true king nted by YHWH—and hated him with satanic, derous hatred. Have you ever pondered how it is Satan still perseveres in unleashing his energy on s people, even as he knows full well that he cannot What makes him waste his power and brilliance something so catastrophically, eternally, and ously futile? He is the epitome of double-dedness, and so those who bear his image resemble in that way. When folks deal with demigods, they can drive themselves crazy trying to determine ther or not the person knows what they are doing. answer is both that they do, and that they do not. Law is written on their hearts so that they are out excuse, even as God has given them over to the futility of their minds. Even so, these folks will often restrain their sin around many or even most people, revealing that they do know they're sinning, and they can control it when they want to. Again, one only has to contemplate the stunning foolishness of the enemy of our souls, and then come to grips with the fact that those who worship him (and according to the Bible, that is most people) will become like him, in order to make sense of the way these people think and behave.

If you lack wisdom as you interact with someone like this, you will help them (and the enemy) perpetuate their lies. If you commit yourself to doing one simple thing—namely, to refuse to lie to yourself and do what you can not to help others lie to themselves either—you will draw the person's Saul-like ire: a satanic campaign to destroy you. You will be at the very crux of the cosmic soul war, and it will be far easier in the short term if you tap out rather than persevering in truthfulness.

F ne way, reading one's Bible or sitting under good p ching actually can subserve the enemy's plans b use most folks in the pew do not know how to take v t they learn and apply it to their lives. They assume t learning is the same as growing, and so they b me inoculated to the truth, even while they keep f g their heads with it. Think about Saul, who l ied directly from a prophet of God, intellectually a ed with what he heard, but served Satan with his l He never did get off the fence and commit to one s or the other, which was a choice in itself. Samuel r atedly told Saul in no uncertain terms what he was l and what he needed to do, but Saul wanted what h wanted, was not humble enough to receive i uction, and blasted forward as if he and not God v the center of the universe.

I u try to help terminally double-minded folks see a nconsistency between what God wants for them, v they intellectually ascribe to, and how they live, y often will incur their wrath, even if it's only in the form of retreat or withdrawal. Just look at Saul's life. And Pharaoh's, and Nebuchadnezzar's, and Judas's. Judas even felt badly for his sin and called it what God calls it, just like Saul did.

God's people are characterized by not only knowing but living consistently in that knowledge. Satan's people, most people, will pour out hatred and deception on them and about them. The pattern of interaction between the two is lived out over and over again, day by day, in the lives of everyday Christians in the church. Within the church, Satan masquerades as an angel of light and is, on paper at least, for everything God is for and against everything God is against, but he rails against those who are fully committed to truth.

If someone sees behind the mask, though, and seeks to serve them with the truth, will they see that person as faithful or as a threat? The difficult part of all of this is that folks who genuinely are Christ's won't always respond well to correction at first. If you persevere with them, sometimes over the course of years and years, t will sometimes come to their senses and repent. I mpossible to know who is who most of the time, a often serving them is just too incredibly difficult a taxing, so the would-be helpers give up and let t retreat into their deception. When this happens, a v s chalked up in the enemy's column. That is not to s hat you must keep every too-big person in your l out do realize what's at stake here. Truth telling is t mmune system of any group of people, and for s any church, and neglecting it will have a price tag f eyond what you can imagine. Yes, the short-term c is steep as well; remember, though, that our Lord p ised us trouble in this world. If you try to c mvent trouble, you'll eventually still get it in a v e form as the deception metastasizes and grows f ore deadly.

I you ever been devastated when someone you l ed up to fell catastrophically, when God had t endously used them in your life? You shouldn't h to look any farther than Saul to understand how this could be the case. God lavishly gifted Saul and used him greatly. Satan is the ultimate example of wicked giftedness, used by God to highlight His own goodness. Satan is the great deceiver, the great perverter of truth, and is also the instrument by which God is displaying His perfect justice, so in that sense even Satan is being greatly used by God for His own glory. This interaction is reenacted in miniature a billion times a day, and each of these interactions has eternal significance.

In the context of ministry, I have at times had the opportunity to peek behind the scenes at Christian public figures and see that, like the Wonderful Wizard of Oz, the man behind the curtain is often vastly different than the larger-than-life image on the screen. The man (or woman) may pontificate on the Word with uncanny skill and insight, and may be a tyrant at home. He may turn a clever phrase in such a way that he gains the fawning admiration of the masses and become so addicted to that admiration that it fuels his desire to still more in selfish ambition, to the praise of his glorious grace. His wife may not be able to stand ight of him anymore, but the pretty lady in the pew sees his true worth. Is it really so difficult to ow a catastrophic fall can come about?

this week, Facebook showed me a picture of an y-year-old former rock star and his hot young In the article accompanying the picture, the ig woman was quoted as saying that what the two em had was true love. She didn't even know the was worth 500 million dollars when she met him! ;ine her surprise. Now, the guy is not stupid. He vs that men his age are not attractive to women like vife. He knows this as well as any sane person ing the article does. But his view of himself has fueled for years by screaming fans and phantic reporters, so that he truly has come to ve the lie that he is special. Maybe most genarians are not sexy, but he's not most genarians. Do you not think this can happen in the church? Is Saul, or his spiritual mentor Satan for that matter, really that tough to understand?

Think about the churchgoing man who is an excellent Sunday school teacher, but who is a spiritual non-entity in the home. Let's say his wife wants nothing more than for him to love and lead her, and for him to pour into their kids, for heaven's sake, but he checks out after work and vegges on YouTube videos instead of engaging with the family God gave him to love and shepherd. Who he is at home is the most accurate representation of who he truly is, even though people at church believe his mask. The result is that they unwittingly help him lie to himself. Is he going to believe his wife's testimony about him, or his fans'? Even if the wife is not being as helpful as she could be in bringing correction, if he had a teaspoon of wisdom he would take her words—and GOD's WORDS—to heart and repent. As soon as he begins to see himself as a victim of this dripping faucet of a woman, the enemy's work is all but finished.

r this guy's version of the rockstar's wife: a lovely
ıg barista, raised by a single mom, hungry for
ership and stability, who laughs at all of his jokes
vorks hard to get his coffee just right. Both of them
each other, and both knowingly and willingly
ent to being used, whether they keep their
ionship in fantasy land or they consummate it in
hysical world. They love the lie more than the
, because to them, the benefits of falsehood far
eigh the enduring pain of doing the hard but good
s that will lead them to true peace, joy, and
ity. Esau made the same mistake, and the Lord
not grant him repentance even though he sought it
tears. That's a terrifying thought, yes? When does
ipping point occur between when repentance is
possible for a person, and when he has been
ered permanently recalcitrant? God's goodness
bestow either retributive irony or redemptive
on these folks; they will get either the thing they
rve, in all of its implication, as a foretaste of the
ment to come, or they will get an exquisitely

crafted trial, the purpose of which is intended to drive them to the Savior and make them like Him. More than likely, both will suffer and rail at God as if it were His fault (Proverbs 19:3).

Please don't hear me say that everything that happened to this hypothetical young woman was her fault, by the way. To some extent, she couldn't know what she didn't know, especially with respect to having had no positive male influences. In a sense, it would be almost impossible for her to choose a man wisely. Still, though, she is not innocent. All of us need both wisdom and holiness that we don't have, and we are accountable to God for our own sin.

If you offer any immature person the choice between some flimsy reward now and treasure five years from now, they will take immediate gratification every time, and they may even be jealous of the folks who have the prize that they themselves forsook. Do you think that it must be nice to be as good at playing piano as your friend is, even though you chose to play outside instead acticing like she did when you were kids? You may h at a viral video of a five-year-old who chooses to the pack of gum he can see and have right now at xpense of some really valuable gift offered to him, ided he wait three years, but are you choosing the the good, and the beautiful, day in and day out, king immediate superficial social blessings, in r to gain what truly matters, even if you won't see ayoff until the eternal state?

you committed never to lie to yourself, Friend? Do surround yourself with people who are willing to nd you, or do you feel victimized by godly friends? susceptible are you to flattery? Your answers to questions may well reveal whether you are a of God, or if you are like your father the devil.

you willing to tell people what they need to hear, ng receiving their hatred in return? What do you you will wish you had done when your life is over? Do you think your choice matters for you for eternity?

If a young lady is consumed with wanting to move to Africa and be a missionary because she says she wants to tell people about Jesus, but she rarely if ever shares the gospel where she is now, do not sign off on her plans. If she chooses to be a fool, let her do so with your loving concerns still ringing in her ears.

If a man wants to be a street evangelist but his marriage is a mess, what might the true motives for his aspirations be, even if he can't or won't admit to them? What potential—or dare I say inevitable—downfalls can you see to him pursuing ministry outside his home at this point in his life? I suspect that one way Satan attacks the church is to identify gifts in young believers, and then influence folks to promote them before they possess the requisite character.

Saul was given to Israel as king as a form of retributive irony, as we discussed in the last chapter. He got the position without the needed character and maturity,

… God's people paid dearly for their foolishness. God … made David king, but He granted him persecution …ng to maturity before He allowed him actually to … the throne. Just like Saul, David gravely sinned, … he repented when confronted. David leaves you …dering how someone so gifted can be so very …sh, but he depended on the grace we all need so … he laid hold of a righteousness not his own. His …ding before God was provided by the true and …ter David, the sinless Son of God Himself.

…d pursued truth in his inward parts, not perfectly …ruly. The trajectory of his life was characterized by …ejection of falsehood. Not so for Saul. Saul wanted …s help enough to sin to get it, pursuing a witch to … him raise Samuel from the dead. He did not, …ever, want it enough to humble himself and get it …od's terms. From Saul, through Saul, and to Saul … all things. In Saul's mind, he was good, and what …id was good, irrespective of what YHWH said. …VH was useful to Saul's plans, no doubt, but He most certainly was not LORD and God. Saul tried to bend reality to suit himself, while David, through persecution and pain, learned to yield to God. Saul's big, seemingly humble words were empty and they did not fool David for a moment. David recognized that Saul did not seek God while He may be found, and that YHWH had given Saul over. David would not mete out judgment, but he recognized that the Lord's judgment on Saul was imminent because Saul found no place for repentance.

Can you spot the difference between repentance and deception in yourself and others? Will you ask the Lord to help you worship Him in spirit and in truth, and to give you eyes to see, ears to hear, and a heart that understands? Those who worship idols, remember, have eyes that don't see, ears that don't hear, and hearts that don't perceive. A person with cancer can eat and eat and still waste away, and a person with spiritual cancer is similar. Don't fool yourself into thinking that spiritual intake, either in yourself or others, is a good t ; in itself unless it yields the fruit of the Spirit in y life. How much truth can you bear hearing about y self, even from sources you do not prefer? Do you v to be like Christ, or do you want admiration, r ect, adoration? What is the effect of your life on the p le closest to you? Please take time to reflect at l h and prayerfully about each of these questions. If y are blind, you never know when your blindness v become permanent and irreversible.

I ow hundreds of Christians, and I don't think I k v ten people who would recognize that Saul was a f if they met him in the wild. As I contemplate the e atological deception Paul told the Thessalonians to e ct, I wonder if this is it. More than ever, we live in a e where "encourage one another" is the ultimate i ul care, and "rebuke one another" (1 Timothy 5:20, 2 nothy 4:2, Titus 1:9, Titus 1:13) is only valid to e oy when someone is, well, rebuking people. Since c spiritual immune system is compromised in this way, even genuine Christians often attack healthy Body "tissue" while they allow disease to spread unchecked.

This means that if you are persecuted by a Saul-like, too-big, demigod type of person, you may not get much help or sympathy. When you choose to stand for truth rather than lies, you may well stand alone and be subjected to relentless persecution from all sides. What should you do if this is the case?

David blessed the one who was persecuting him, warring not against the man but against the enemy of his soul. He was impervious to manipulation. He did not exalt himself or succumb to self-pity, and remained in exile, to his own inconvenience and discomfort, even knowing that he himself was the rightful king. He waited on the Lord to make things right, but he didn't neglect his own responsibilities at any time, including speaking very clearly regarding Saul's wickedness. When there was no man to lead David, he led himself and his men in truth, courage, and faithfulness. As much as David sinned later on, these things and not the re what defined him, what made him the man after 's own heart. As you suffer unjustly, how much do resemble David? He was the victim, but he did not a victim mentality, and so he became fit to rule s people equitably. Are you like David, and like rue and greater David, when Satan attacks you? If are not, what does God want you to do right now?

g in David's position is not desirable in one sense, hen again biblical blessedness has sometimes been ied as "the enviable position of divine favor," and beatitudes say that we are blessed when we are ed, persecuted, and falsely spoken against in evil. of those who seek to live godly lives will be ecuted. Do you want a life of peace with everyone, life of divine favor? What may your faithfulness ire of you, and is it worth it to you? Does your life the gaze and ire of the evil one, as well as the ed gaze of the Lord? Take comfort, Christian, ving that trials of this kind frequently come to the y, and also that He who is in you is greater than he who is in the world. Love God, love others, tell the truth, and know that the Lord is with you. If you do this, you will be able to say with David, the satanically persecuted man of God:

O LORD, my heart is not lifted up;
my eyes are not raised too high;
I do not occupy myself with things
too great and too marvelous for me.
But I have calmed and quieted my soul,
like a weaned child with its mother;
like a weaned child is my soul within me.

Psalm 131:1–2

7

Introduction to Part II

I ıese last few pages, I have included some case s ıes to help us move from theory into practice in our c ıderation of more extreme cases of too-big people. (› again, each of us thinks more highly of ourselves t we ought, so we should seek to apply the scalpel (e Word to our own hearts first. On the other hand, a e have also discussed, some folks do not operate (›od faith or in consideration of others as a rule, and v ıust think carefully about how to serve and live v them.

/ ice as it would be to have a flow chart teaching us h to respond to manipulative people in every p ible situation, that approach would not truly be h ful because we must always base our decisions and r ions upon what honors God, which is always more a ıt the motives for our actions than it is about the actions themselves. What would be the best thing for the demigod-like person in the moment? Would overlooking their sin be a gracious way not to overwhelm them? Maybe so, if they genuinely are making an effort to change. Also, you can't call out every little thing someone does wrong. Often, overlooking someone's sin does more to help them lie to themselves, though, and contributes to the hardening of their hearts. You must use God-given wisdom in each and every moment of all your relationships. Do what you can not to help them lie to themselves, and not to let their sin go unchecked, always with their good in mind. Sometimes, distancing yourself from them when possible is the best road for everyone. Having to navigate these things ourselves is the way God works in us to produce humility and wisdom, and so to provide checklists would circumvent that process, removing the responsibility each of us has to consider the person in front of us, cry out to God for help, and make the most loving choice we can, given our limitations. Failure, repentance,

ing, and growth are also necessary parts of this ess.

of the truths I wanted to communicate in the three studies is that you acting faithfully toward one does not necessarily lead to them responding If someone is crying and claims to have been nized, that does not mean they are right. If you d up to someone who is very self-righteous and ature, you probably will wish you hadn't. They had much practice in punishing anyone who ld dare to challenge them, and their punishment has been effective to protect them from intability. The health of their soul depends on change, and their change depends upon them g themselves clearly, which they probably won't ble to do without help. Also, letting them sin nst you or others with impunity isn't good for them nore than it is good for you.

wanted to show you what a godly response could like. The case studies are good examples of possible scenarios, based upon my own experiences with overbearing and demanding folks. I'm related to some, I've counseled some, and I'm friends with some. According to secular data, these folks do not change. Worldly sources do not understand the power of the Spirit of God, though. Having said that, it still is rare for a profoundly self-absorbed person to humble herself enough to cry out to the Lord for true repentance. I've seen it, but not often. Faithfulness that came with a guaranteed good response would be easier, no doubt, but faithfulness in a situation that may well never change has a profoundly deeper value. Only if you are committed to honoring our *a se,* impassible God and bearing His image in the face of adversity can you ever hope to persevere through such a trial.

Having said that, I pray these vignettes are a blessing to you.

8

Case Study 1: Lamia

Hush now, baby, baby, don't you cry

ımma's gonna make all of your nightmares come true

Mamma's gonna put all of her fears into you

lamma's gonna keep you right here, under her wing

She won't let you fly, but she might let you sing

Mamma's gonna keep baby cosy and warm

Of course, Mamma's gonna help build the wall

Pink Floyd

excellent wife is the crown of her husband, but she who ımes him is like rottenness in his bones. Proverbs 12:4

I ia is a middle-aged woman whose beauty is past i ›rime and for whom life has brought many (›pointments. Years ago, her then ten-year-old (;hter Megan died of leukemia and Lamia never r ›ered from the shock of the loss. The truism "there is no sorrow as deep as the loss of a child; there is no love as deep as a mother's" has been repeated over and over again in her household, but some in the family have long since begun to wonder how the heartache of living with a selfish woman who has lost a child compares to Lamia's pain, even though no one would dare ask the question out loud. Her surviving children are adults now and have begun to start families of their own, further adding to her grief as they don't need her like they once did. In fact, they call her less and less, and she feels victimized by their inattention.

Over the years, her husband became increasingly quiet and withdrawn. In the early days after Megan's death, he did everything he could to make Lamia happy and quell her insecurities, but eventually he realized he was trying to do the impossible. He eventually became a nonentity in his family, full of anger he didn't express out loud, secretly indulging in several vices to help quiet the noise in his soul. He saw, much too late, that he had made the world revolve around his wife, first use of her youthful beauty, later because of her ring, until at last he had created a monster he saw ope of ever taming. He was fully aware that he was f Lamia's many disappointments but didn't know e to begin to change, or even what needed to ge. He noticed that she was flirty with other men, he hoped she will just leave him so he could have chance at happiness. Some other poor sucker's would be his gain, with any luck at all. He believed od, was a beloved deacon in his church, but how d he lead a wife like his? Lamia's overbearing re was apparent to nearly everyone, and most folks adly for him, which kept them from confronting ulpability in the family's problems.

ears after the tragedy, most of Lamia's maternal y was focused on her son Seth who was 16 when ster died. Seth was disappointed by his dad's lack adership, so he did what he could to support his in her grief. He believed that her desire to control and know where he was at all times was natural and understandable to a huge extent. When he did become exasperated by her manipulation, the tears in her lovely, hurting eyes melted his heart and he relented into compliance.

When he was 21, Seth finally moved out of his parents' home when he married Daphne. He fell in love with Daphne because of her love for the Lord, her vivacious joy, and the relative normalcy of her family compared to his. Naturally, his wife and mother did not get along well, and it took Seth quite a while to see that Daphne's concerns about his mom's interference in their life were serious and valid. Daphne was not an enemy to his family as he had been tempted at times to think she was, or as his mom claimed she was when she would whisper in his ear about Daphne's supposed self-righteousness. Daphne did struggle with sinful anger toward Lamia, but Daphne's deepest desire truly was to honor the Lord and love Lamia well, as difficult as that was to do, so Seth committed himself to protecting his new family by not allowing his mother to overstep l)ounds. Seth and Daphne soon were expecting a c ;hter, whom Lamia wanted them to name Megan. S)ecame persistent in her pleas, and Seth knew he r : act. Seth and Daphne were part of a good church, a ıe asked his elders to help him honor the Lord, his v , and his mom as he prepared to navigate what he k v full well would be a tumultuous time.

/ ıe birth of his daughter approached, Seth began i ersing himself in the study of God's character and r re. He knew that if he were to withstand the storm t ıme, he would need to be firmly grounded as the l 's image bearer, particularly with respect to His i ıssibility. He had to do what was right without b ; controlled by his mother's anger, tears, or other f s of manipulation. Also, he had to work through h ıpbringing with the Lord, rejecting any form of a r at God, including self-pity for what he went t ıgh. The Lord had brought Seth both the gift of life a the gift of suffering (Philippians 1:29), and Seth v determined to live in gratitude for God's kindness to him. Instead of viewing his wife as a competitor, he wisely saw her as his greatest ally and the two of them committed to doing what was best for the other.

Seth began his new ministry to his family by lovingly addressing his father, confronting him about his lack of leadership. Seth did not speak in anger, nor did he proffer any ultimatums. Instead, he told his dad about his plan to limit Lamia's influence in his new family's life, and told him he would primarily direct his communication through him after an initial conversation with Lamia in which he would reassure her of his love and confront her longstanding sin pattern. He offered his help and advice to his father if he wanted it, understanding that his dad did not know how to proceed, but also making sure he knew God expected him to make an effort toward loving his wife and leading her well. Dad was not happy, but he said that he understood and would respect his son's wishes.

Seth and Daphne's daughter was born in early November. They had been prayerfully considering to handle the approaching holidays, given that expected a conflict to ensue during their first ly gathering after Seth's conversations with his nts. His mother had chosen to react quietly and cally to her son's words, retreating from the entire ly for two months before inviting everyone to her e for Thanksgiving. Her only reply had been to nent to Seth that now she had lost two children ad of one, and her granddaughter as well. He told hat wasn't true, that she was in control of how n she saw them, and if she would walk in love and ility toward his wife, they could all have a derful relationship.

and Daphne accepted the invitation to ksgiving dinner with reasonable expectations for the day would go. It began well, with everyone lly making over the new baby and catching up on nother's lives. Eventually, though, the mood took xpected downturn when Lamia made a snide nent about not having been invited to the baby's birth. Seth gently corrected her, but she continued to pout, so he kissed her on the head, told her he loved her, gathered his family, and left. His calm demeanor dissolved on the way home and he wept with grief, and Daphne wept with him. When they got back to the house, they worshipped God together, thanked Him for loving and leading them, and ate the food they had prepared in advance, knowing they would likely need it.

As Christmas approached, Seth fasted for a few days in prayer for his family. He reached out to his dad to decline his mother's invitation, reiterating his love for them and his desire for them to repent and honor the Lord. He and Daphne spent the holiday with her family, rejoicing in the Lord and in the opportunity to be faithful to Him and enjoy making new traditions together. Seth's siblings were struggling to understand his choices, but he rested his heart in God's kindness, knowing that the Lord could be trusted with his reputation, and also with the well-being of his beloved f ly. He treated each of them graciously as he i acted with them, but did not feel the need to e ain himself endlessly. When bitterness toward a ne—including one another at times-- crept into t hearts, Seth and Daphne confessed it to God and b ed for His help to change.

I nuary, Seth and Daphne dropped in on Lamia for h irthday. They brought her flowers, let her hold the b , and didn't stay long. Daphne's birthday was in F uary, and she received a passive aggressive text f her mother-in-law that day, so after prayerful c ideration, Seth reached out to his dad to let him k v that they would be blocking Lamia on his wife's p e. They had no contact with the family for several r ths. During that time, Seth began to realize how r n more clearly and biblically he was thinking since l amily's influence over him had lessened. He was g ful for the chance to raise his own family c rently than he had been raised, and became more c nitted than ever not to let anything interfere with the emotional and spiritual well-being of Daphne and their children.

Seth's dad slowly took up the challenge to protect his family from his wife, and to ask God to let her experience the joy and freedom of a clean conscience. When Lamia began crying loudly at the family's Mother's Day gathering the following year, railing about Seth and Daphne, her husband corrected her in front of everyone. He asked for his kids' forgiveness for his lack of courage and protection, and asked them all to join with him and Seth in bringing care to Lamia.

Over time, he fostered a relationship with a good group of guys at church with whom he gathered for breakfast every Saturday. He had to teach them not to encourage his hatred of his wife, but to faithfully hold him accountable to be the man God wants him to be. His wife hadn't changed much, but oddly, he had hope in Christ for the first time in his life. He was able to help a few young guys get off to a good start in leading their

\ s, which was an unexpected but immense
k ness from the Lord.

S is away from his extended family more than he's
i ntact with them now. He loves them more than
e but he knows he's doing something radical in
g ıg himself to learning, loving, and leading his own
\ , and he can't allow them to hinder what God
c d him to do. The road he's chosen is a hard one,
b ıe knows all too well that the alternative is much,
r h harder. What his mother selfishly demanded
f her family, she could freely and easily have
(ined through humility, but as of yet she remains
l l to that fact. Seth's kids will know a better way, by
t race of God.

9

Case Study 2: Niobe

I don't want to argue about who is the victim
'Cause maybe we both got burned
I don't want to talk about who is the traitor
'Cause both of our loyalties turned
I don't want to fight about who is the liar
'Cause there's too many ways to lie
I don't want to hear about who is the winner
'Cause we both know it's a tie
Cut it out, drop it, count me out, baby stop it
Life is too short, so why waste precious time

Pat Benatar

Niobe was always on the outside looking in. She grieved in silence when she saw others laughing, talking, crying, and praying together after the church service, and she wondered what was wrong with her that no one drew her in. Isn't the church supposed to r outcasts and misfits, she thought? Couldn't they hat she had a lot to offer? Why would no one give chance?

e's church was a good one, for the most part. The le noticed and cared about Niobe, but they found o be closed off, so that if a kind lady attempted to ge her in conversation, the lady would have to essly think of questions to ask if the conversation to continue. The general perception of Niobe was she wasn't overly interested in having friends, h wasn't true, but people couldn't know what they 't know. Folks eventually gave up and moved on, ıe most part. Niobe responded by being even more rdly curved, fearing the rejection she was sure she ld receive, which became a self-fulfilling prophecy rts.

e's husband had been raised by an overbearing ıer, and as a young man, he basked in the attention eautiful and charming fiancé lavished upon him. they were married, though, he found that nothing he did seemed to be enough to please his wife. She cried easily, and he spent his days and years trying unsuccessfully to make her happy. As their kids grew, so did their insecurities, as living in an emotionally volatile home caused them constantly to wonder whether they would be met with love and affection or anger and tears in response to their frantic efforts to be good kids and not upset anyone. They didn't understand that their parents and not they themselves were the problem, so they worked and slaved toward a goal they would never achieve. When their work didn't pay off, they retreated into video games, and then later into secret sexual sin, and finally alcohol use, to dull the pain. They eventually began to show signs of resentment, to which Niobe responded in self-pity, which made the kids feel guilty and increasingly angry.

When Niobe complained to her husband about the kids, and about her treatment at the hands of the church ladies, he knew his wife was probably most of problem because he had suffered under her ment, and he knew from observation that the ıen Niobe was struggling with were kind, joyful, servant hearted. As for the kids, well, who was the t here? He dismissed those thoughts quickly, gh, knowing that no matter how kindly he nunicated them, they would not be received well. lid not have the courage to walk her through her sin and discontentment, so instead he, too, loped a low-grade anger toward their church ly for failing them. Why wouldn't at least one of godly ladies pursue his wife? Isn't that what the ch is supposed to do? Help a brother out, here.

other reason why it was difficult to hold Niobe untable for her sin was that when she complained m and he empathized with her, expressing anger he way she was neglected, he became her hero ı, even if briefly, and a glimpse of the old magic back. He lived for those moments like a junkie for his next fix. He often felt himself drawn seemingly helplessly into a fascination with porn, but having her look at him the way she did when he commiserated with her struggles made his lust battle a bit easier for a time. On one level, he knew he was helping her lie to herself, but he wasn't willing to stand up to her, get real help, and work toward a genuine solution. He lacked the courage, humility, and wisdom to do what Niobe needed him to do and so he became the other side of the victim coin.

Briefly, a few years previously, they did go to a few counseling sessions, but when Niobe's beautiful eyes filled with tears and her lip began to quiver, the counselor was so moved by chivalry and a desire to protect her that he, like Niobe's husband, failed to protect her from her selfishness and reinforced it instead. "Every man reacts to her that way," he thought angrily. He himself was "every man," but he chose not to think about that. It was easier to blame everyone but himself for his problems.

N e's husband did a good job hiding his anger and v out of his way to be helpful at church. His elders c d see how difficult Niobe could be at times, and s him as a stand-up guy. They felt badly for him, so t offered him a position as a deacon, which he g ly accepted. He loved being recognized. Lots of f at church began noticing and commenting on his h fulness, which fueled his problems and angered N e. She didn't respect him to begin with, and she c ted the attention he was getting, so their home life v from bad to worse.

S etimes at church, Niobe noticed a white-haired v an watching her. When their eyes met, the lady—M rva, or Minnie as she was called—smiled softly a kindly. Niobe simultaneously felt drawn to and a d of Minnie, and she wasn't sure why. As she b n to watch Minnie in return, Niobe saw that many p le didn't seem to notice the old woman at all, v e several approached her regularly, with serious a reverent faces, and seemed to hang on her every word. She was content, calm, and observant when she was alone, focused and engaged when talking to others. Minnie was bent over with what appeared to be severe arthritis, but joy and not pain was written on her face. Interesting.

One day, Niobe's husband unexpectedly came home early from work, and she used that opportunity to take some "me time." Wishing she had a friend to meet, Niobe freshened her lipstick, grabbed her purse and a novel, and headed out alone to a local coffee shop. When she walked in, she noticed two women at a table in the corner: a young, plain woman with a sad but radiant smile on her face, and Minnie. As Niobe ordered her coffee, the young woman stood, embraced Minnie firmly, and turned to leave. When the young woman reached her car, Minnie appeared to be praying. A pang of jealousy pierced Niobe's heart. She collected her latte, found an unoccupied corner booth, and sat down to read.

' ˌbe." The older woman stood before her a short
\ e later. "Minnie. From church." Her eyes were
ed, probably leftover from her previous encounter,
t she smiled sweetly. Niobe acted surprised to see
h and smiled in return.

N e was elated by the older woman's gesture, and
s offered her a seat. Starved for friendship, Niobe
t d and talked, eventually telling all of her woes to
t woman she instinctively trusted. She remarked at
l on her own loneliness and longing to have what
N nie had in the form of deep relationships. Finally,
s topped talking.

T Minnie spoke.

*en I was young, I wasn't pretty like you are. I wasn't
irt. There was nothing to make me stand out, which I
w now was a gift, because I didn't have much to make
think I was better than anybody else. When my daddy
't drunk, he was telling me I was stupid and worthless,
believed him. Not in a self-pitying way, I just thought
ier people were more important than I was and that I
ed to serve them. Turns out that that's what Jesus said
uld think about myself, so we were on the same page in*

that way before I formally knew Him. I don't know why He was so kind to grant that to me, but He was.

My husband was a selfish, mean man. The only time I ever was pregnant, he hit me so hard that I lost the baby. I called the police and he went to jail for a year; I spent two weeks in the hospital alone. During that time, I couldn't afford our mortgage, so we lost the house. I became a nanny so I would have a place to live, babies to love, and food to eat while I waited for him to get out. When he did get out, he didn't dare hit me again, which was nice, but he blamed me for everything that happened and my life didn't get any better. In all of that time, I was so lonely.

But the Lord opened my eyes to the fact that everyone around me was lonely. I was waiting for someone to notice me and love me, and so was most everybody else, which made me excited, because I got an idea. I started asking people at church random questions in order to draw them out and get to know them a little better, and before long I always had people around me.

After this had been going on for a while, I started to feel like I was drowning and bleeding in shark infested waters, while throwing as many life preservers as I could to the people around me. Some folks clung to me for dear life, threatening to drown us both. Others sat on the shore with their backs to me, sad or angry that I wasn't doing enough for them. The angry ones threw things at me, which didn't help me or them. But there were a precious few who took the life preservers and used them well. They got out and started helping me and others, and for their sakes it was all worth ı a sense, my life got harder and lonelier, but there was 'emn blessedness from the Lord that helped me endure. t turned out, the thing I wanted most was found where people don't want to look for it, but the Lord led me to Him and love others and I couldn't be more thankful to Him for that.

n Niobe got home, she couldn't contain her tears longer. Her alarmed husband asked what was ıg (THIS time, he thought, but didn't say), so she him about her encounter with Minnie.

e was literally my last hope, and she made the whole ersation about herself. I think she meant for her story to e some kind of passive aggressive dig at me, and she esn't even know me! How dare she judge a wounded ɔn like that! That's the last straw—I'm not setting foot in that church again.

years later, clad in a plain dress and no makeup, e sat down in the back pew for Minnie's funeral. had almost chosen to wear sunglasses, but there ı't much chance anyone would recognize her so she went *sans* disguise. From her vantage point, she could see a modest gathering of people laughing through tears, hugging one another, and trying to lighten one another's burdens through their own heartbreak. A few seemed to be in despair, likely wondering what they would ever do without Minnie. What would it be like, she wondered, to leave such a void when you die? Niobe's husband had left her a year before for his high school sweetheart, and the kids went with him. She had been able to guilt the kids into coming to her apartment on the weekends for the first few months after the separation, but eventually they stopped answering her calls. Why fight in court for people who didn't want to spend time with you? Even if she had won, what kind of victory would that have been? For years, she had wanted nothing more than a break from her kids; now she had it.

As she lay awake at night in those first terrible months, the Lord wouldn't let her escape the fact that she had never loved her husband. She'd loved that he loved her, h of course was not the same thing. The hurt she feeling was because she thought she deserved r, just for being who she was (*and who was that?* she wondered), not because of missing someone she d for. That man had just been to her a bit player in tory of her own life. All hail Queen Niobe. Maybe is time to start telling herself the truth, and just be one of Minnie's spiritual kids could help her see ly if she would humble herself and ask. It occurred r as certainly as she knew her own name that if she not take this opportunity, she wouldn't be granted her. *Lord, help.*

10

Preface to Case Study 3

In the case of you who have never directly experienced the sinful persecution of the type of person I am calling a demigod, I wanted to give you an idea of what it is like so that you have a chance to bring compassionate and effective care to those who have. The most difficult thing for recipients of this type of behavior is that almost no one understands it, so attempts at helping frequently do more harm than good. I also want to serve you by bringing needed self-clarity, on the chance that you may be sinning against someone in the way I'm describing.

I heard once that you can make a dog starve itself to death if you smack it on the nose with a newspaper fifty times in a row when it tries to approach its food dish. After that, it won't try to eat anymore and it will eventually die.

\ t if you also smacked it for every minor
i ıvenience to yourself? *That didn't bother me last*
but it does today because I didn't sleep well. Smack!
\ t if you decide you feel badly for what you've done
a you're no longer going to smack the dog for eating,
a then you get angry at it for not eating, so you
s :k it again? What if you actually feel victimized by
t act that it won't eat, as if it's being unfair to you
s :how by starving to death in front of you? If you've
r r lived with this kind of treatment, it will rightly
s shocking to you, but it many cases, this is the way
t too-big people operate. The folks that live with
t may be the only ones experiencing them this way,
a ıe demigod type will often put on a charming
f le to impress others, but in private the recipients of
t foul treatment live in a world where they cannot
c nything to gain the favor of their loved one. The
t :t is impossible to obtain, but they will still be
p shed if they don't wear themselves out trying to
r ı it.

Now imagine that it's not a dog that's being treated that way, but your spouse, child, or friend. Man or woman, are you a nag? Do you bite and devour the people in your life? Do you expect relational blessings from them, even when you won't repent for your relentless sin against them?

What if you want an attractive wife, so you subtly punish her when she eats more than you think she should? You don't want to be a jerk, right? So you don't actually tell her what you're thinking, but you still want to make sure she knows. You are a subtle and creative communicator, all the while maintaining plausible deniability. What if she is attractive, and does what you want her to in order to remain so, so that others notice and admire her beauty? Do you ever tear her down to make sure she won't think too highly of herself? Will you disdain her if she then gets discouraged and lets herself go?

Wife, are you impossible to please?

ow I'm tough to live with, but I have a lot on my mind you can't possibly understand that. Yes, I hit you on nose fifteen times today with a newspaper for no good n and I ignore you unless I want something from you, I'm still struggling with the way you didn't serve me ectly two months ago. It really hurt and it shows that don't care for me as much as you should. You have no to be afraid of me because your fear makes me feel bad, ich isn't fair. I need you to respond as if you've been l and cherished your entire life, even though I probably 't change a whole lot. If you understood what I've been rough you'd have more grace for me. I know I'm not ct, but nothing's good enough for you. You completely look all the good things I do for you. You really need to let go of this unforgiving spirit you have.

I s is you, well, you probably won't know it. If you c ee it and are willing to acknowledge it, that a owledgment likely will not translate into change, v h is the hardest and saddest part for me about v ng this book. Curved inward people, as I said b re, are idolators, and as such they have eyes that c t see, ears that don't hear, and hearts that don't u rstand. *I am good, and what I do is good.* Lord v ng, some readers are not too far gone yet, and so they will read this and repent while there's time. This book is mostly for the ones who see a problem in someone they care about and want to help, though. If you know someone like the person I'm describing, don't let your misguided compassion make you fall for the pity party. If you're counseling a couple with this dynamic in their relationship from either spouse, the manipulative person will play you like a fiddle if you're not wise. You'll be his tool, and you will help him make his family's life even more miserable.

Now, if you read all of this and you're saying, "YES!! This is exactly what happened to me!" my heart goes out to you, because that's an unbelievably hard way to live. Don't respond by curving inward, though, whatever you do, because you might be in danger of perpetuating the problem if you fall into a victim mentality as a result.

Let me illustrate. Let's say there is a family—father, mother, son—and the dad is angry and selfish. Mom understandably becomes distraught because she's erned about the effects that her husband's anger have on her son, so she makes it her life's goal to l up what her husband has torn down. She does ything she can to make sure her boy knows he is d and special. If he's down, she takes him on a ial outing. She'll do without something she wants eds in order to give him the tennis shoes that will him not stand out as inferior to the kids at school. t have anyone look down on HER boy; he's been igh enough. She'll talk to the teachers at school to them aware of the situation at home so that they have extra patience for her son, and so they will sure he's always treated fairly.

lashes out in anger toward another student and ther kid's parents come talk to her, she will explain he's acting out because he's been mistreated ch he hears, by the way, and knows he's off the for his sin). *It's not his fault, really. I'm sure you rstand.* When he's selfish, pouty, and demanding rd other kids, causing them to exclude him, she cries with him and talks about how cruel kids can be. Then she takes him for ice cream to cheer him up. She didn't mean to, but she's created an insufferable little drama king, all the while thinking she's the best thing to ever happen to him. No human being loves him as much as she does, which is the absolute truth, and she genuinely is doing the best she can much of the time, but she is blind to the fullness of reality, which is that her influence on him is absolutely destructive. She sees his selfishness, no doubt, but her diagnosis is wrong, and so, therefore, is her prescription.

It is not possible for her to make him feel better because his experiential peace depends upon him getting over himself—learning to love God and others. He gets worse and worse and she tries harder and harder to make it better. She may assume he's having a mental health crisis because of his trauma, because of his angry dad baggage, but she misses the fact that God opposes the proud, and He won't share glory with this budding demigod. He has soul noise, or conscience sorrow, that r manifest itself in any number of ways: anxiety, c ession, etc.

I lentally, God designed you so that the reward c ers of your brain will only be activated if you a mplish something good—if your heart (science) doesn't condemn you. If you hold others a their failures toward you responsible for your lack c ppiness, **you'll be calling evil good and good evil, a punishing them for the consequences you suffer c to your own failure to actively love God and c rs.**

Y can artificially stimulate your brain to reward you f time, but it won't last. You'll be chasing the c cience joy dragon forever unless you take r onsibility before God and others for your own life. (is not passive, and it doesn't glorify Him when y are, either. When you persist in a victim mentality, y experience His goodness in a different way than y would if you were actively loving Him and others. T form of His impassible goodness that will be directed toward you will be designed to get you to move into a place of blessedness, the place where you are bearing His image more properly. The only way this can happen is when you accurately interpret your soul noise and rightly respond (confession *and* repentance) to the sin in your life that is causing your turmoil. Let me be clear: others' sin against you is their responsibility, not yours. Your external suffering is out of your control, but your response may be adding to your suffering. Don't be disheartened by that, because once you know, you can do something about it. You're in the same boat that everyone else is in, in that you are not perfected yet. It's ok.

So, what kind of husband and father is this kid going to be, do you think? Let's say he reaches adulthood, and that a woman sees his sadness, hears his story, and thinks she can help him. The way he looks at her melts her heart, and he sings her praises night and day. If she can just love him the way he deserves to be loved, the his dad never did, she just knows she can help, so nakes a promise till death do us part. She doesn't v it, but she's taking responsibility for his ional well-being like his mom did, and she's in for 1 more than she bargained for. She's allowing him rego his agency, his responsibility and power to do ight thing, so she will not be a blessing to him, no er how good her intentions are. He's miserable use he's selfish, but he'll make his poor wife his egoat for as long as he can.

t happens when this young lady finds out she's ied to a perpetual eleven-year-old who won't take onsibility for anything? He doesn't have low self-m at all; in fact, he's pretty certain he hung the n and she exists to make him happy. What can she

wife starts to address her husband's selfishness, will he respond? How will his mother respond to It doesn't take much insightfulness at all to see the hood that both of them will slap her on the nose with a newspaper for any offense, or none at all. They will imitate the father's sinful selfishness *and blame him for it*. This pattern will likely repeat itself until Jesus comes back unless someone will speak truth into these too-big self-assessments and be willing to face the intense backlash that will undoubtedly come to them as a result.

I must caution you as a potential helper that it's not your job to stop a suffering, fearful woman from destroying her kid. You must not try to override her agency because then you'll be like her, and be part of the problem. She is not powerful enough to destroy him anyway, only to provide the temptation for him to worship himself, which he must choose to do on his own. But are you willing to tell her the truth about herself? She can effect a tremendous and powerful change for her family if she is willing to change her perspective. She most certainly will see your efforts as a newspaper to the snout, as you telling her that yet one more thing is her fault. Are you courageous enough to her see that, no matter how good her intentions she's not helping her boy? Do you love this ıan's future daughter-in-law and grandchildren gh to intervene? If she does hear you, or if her son , she will be eternally grateful to you. But what if doesn't? Can you be ok with that? Can you oach her with genuine heartbreak over all those spaper swats from her cruel husband, but also with courage to help her rightly view her own ribution to the problem?

t if you're the daughter-in-law? The last case study you. I won't be able to answer every single one of questions there, but I trust that the illustration will elpful, particularly in the context of this whole . Honestly, far too many women in these tions will return evil for evil, but if you're rmined to honor God, no matter what, there's a h but blessed road for you to choose.

ıony Esolen, in his book called *No Apologies,* made nteresting observation that is pertinent to our discussion. He said that all of the government nannying we see now started when women were given voting privileges. Naturally, my eyebrows went up when I first read that, but I've come to believe he's right. Before women's suffrage, the government limited itself to mostly protecting life and property, but when suddenly half its contingency was primarily interested in social reform, it grew to meet the demand, never to shrink again. Women stepped up because men had abdicated their responsibilities to serve and protect, no doubt. They had to. But their help created another problem.

All I have to do is think of the picture I saw once of a little boy, all covered with coal dust and with a cigarette hanging out of his mouth, fresh from his live long day of working in the mine, and I want to start writing my congressman to tell him to get his backside in gear and do something. Women started voting and they changed the world for that kid. They even led the charge to outlaw alcohol so the kid's dad would be likely to get off his duff and go to work. Their ts were in the right place, but can we agree that one deed snowballed into another and another, and esults are not at all what they envisioned?

e ladies had an over-realized eschatology, ing that they were trying to rid the world of evil e wrong way, and in their own timing. The gospel only way to make a dent in the evil of the world, it works in the heart, not in cigarettes, alcohol, or mines. And Jesus made it clear that it would ar that evil was winning, even though it's not, He returns and puts things right. Few, not many, certainly not most will be saved; nevertheless, st will be perfectly glorified by His grace and by ustice in the end. Everything sad, as Samwise said, come untrue.

n, the ladies who helped to outlaw many social ills ed good things, and so do our worried momma, overreaching government, and our selfish, olling, over-mothered kid turned husband. Their whys and hows are off the mark, though. Will you help them continue to lie to themselves? Do you love them enough to help them see? You're only one person, but you are a key soldier in the war against evil, right where you are, if you will locate it in the correct place and then step in to speak truth. Satan masquerades as an angel of light, and sometimes he looks like big, beautiful eyes full of tears, begging you to do something. If the owner of those eyes is ever to be free, she needs you to be both wise as a serpent and gentle as a dove. Both.

A woman's heart is the resume for male church leadership for a reason: leading a woman isn't always easy to do. If you can do it, you can do almost anything. Incidentally, don't you dare take on a leadership position if you can't manage your own house. The Lord forbids it. You can force your wife to appear happy and submissive, or she can appear that way in a misguided effort to help build you up, but your conscience won't uiet if either of these is the case because you can't God.

aside, when I was preparing to write this chapter, ived a text prompting me to change my password family tracking app, an app I don't have. Someone p an account in my name, and it was hard as all get o get the company to delete the thing. Everyone I nunicated with ended their correspondence with own version of Chik-Fil-A's "My pleasure," which e safe." When the account finally was deleted, they an email to me asking for feedback. I told them that creepy little website reminded me of the Hotel ornia. No matter how much I said I didn't want service, they kept trying to attach my actual email ess to the account I didn't make and didn't want ould be safe.

nessage is clear: if you exercise your own little slice mniscience and omnipresence over your loved , you can keep them safe! Just ignore that noise in soul, Friends. You're doing nothing other than living in reality: you have anxiety because this is a big, scary world where anything can happen and only YOU can protect your family. Your turmoil is *definitely not* due to the fact that the Lord is bringing heat to your conscience because you're usurping His authority over others' lives, or because you aren't sure He can be trusted to protect them without you. You're just doing what's reasonable and responsible. Now take a Xanax and go to sleep.

Nothing is inherently wrong with using a tracking app for your family. That's not what I'm saying. The sin of anything is always in the why of it, and I'll leave you to tease out the implications of that truth for the app I mentioned, and for you as well. Don't get distracted from my point. But also remember that totalitarian governments and totalitarian families couch their devices in the guise of keeping people safe in a way that greatly overreaches propriety.

It started when women began to run things, but the spirit of well-meaning but ungodly control has p ieated our whole society, such that we don't stand u) bullies, we ban them. Old men don't teach young r to use guns to protect women anymore, so the v ien took over and banned guns. And men. Many of t ien we do have look more like damsels in need of r ie than a kingdom of priests, sent to serve and p ect.

V ieed good men and good women to stand up and t ie truth, to themselves first and most of all, and to t ı others to do the same. You're probably right a t everyone at whom you want to point a finger, but y can't control them. What does God want you to do? V you be faithful to Him, and to the souls of the p le around you? Going back to the dog and r spaper metaphor at the beginning of the chapter, t solution to the problem is not to do away with r spapers. Newspapers aren't going away until the e of the age, and the Bible exists to tell you what to c ntil then. God has given you nothing but truth—y sling and stone, as it were—as your weapon in this age. Will you wield it? He has already given you the victory no matter what your eyes see. The great God-man crushed the snake's head; the serpent IS defeated. Your eyes will deceive you regarding this reality, which is why you must be steadfast, fixing your eyes on the things not everyone can see.

Our fearful mom actually wants you to take her agency away from her to keep her safe: rescue her, protect her, fix everything, make everything right so that she and her boy can just be happy. The problem with this, like I mentioned before, is that these folks' problem is not people and circumstances. If you don't fix their problems to their satisfaction, which you can't, they may well punish you for laying down your life for them. It's admirable, no doubt, to see hurting people and want to help, but you must help wisely. Over and over, the New Testament tells us that we will have trials, often severe, until the Lord returns, and suffering people must view their lives in light of this reality, which most folks are understandably reluctant to do.

our raccoon in a trap again, with a wounded, ring leg and no desire at all for you to touch it. t will you do? You can't *make* people happy, but can point them to the true condition for their iness, if you have the courage and wisdom to do lease know that I don't say that lightly, but you do have a serious choice to make.

can't fix everything today, but you can start telling ruth, making one right decision at a time. Doing so ers more and avails more than you can possibly v or see right now. What I'm asking you to do is , but the "hard" of not doing it is much worse.

ly overreach and government overreach work selves out similarly. Government does more for us ever, but people are increasingly depressed, ous, and angry. To make matters worse, folks tend o vote for the person who wants to get their leg out e trap. Their greatest need is to have their power responsibility back—to relinquish their death grip neir victimhood. Their joy and freedom are theirs for the taking, but they don't want them where they are to be found. The kind of comfort we want most will only be ours when we are glorified, in the new heavens and new earth. There is greater comfort than you realize available here and now, though, down the road of faithfulness.

Dear lady, or dear citizen, I know it's tempting to cling to someone, anyone who will help. But the person who wants to sweep in and make everything better for you, and take responsibility for your happiness, will almost always lead to a retributive reversal, per our earlier discussion. If you don't want the right thing, for the right reasons, and you're not willing to pursue it with the right methods, if you get what you want it will come to you in the form of discipline. We naturally want God and everybody else to move, but He knows that *we* need to move. When we do, we'll still suffer, but we'll suffer with His grace and peace with us, and not with debilitating conscience sorrow. The Lord loves you, Christian, and He gave His Son for you. He's not

t to let you go now. Taste and see that the Lord is
l.

oday, take your son out and help him clean up an
ly neighbor's yard. Teach him to ask his friends
questions to get to know them better: *What's the*
nd worst things that happened to you today? How may
for you? What's your favorite childhood memory? The
tions don't matter much; you will only be looking
t your kid's eyes off himself, which he won't want
, most likely, and he won't change quickly. You
model what you want him to be, and you must
ely lead him. He needs you far more than he needs
pastor or anyone else, and your faithfulness to
matters.

for and extend forgiveness regularly. Laugh at
self, and teach him to do the same. Teach him how
n and lose graciously. If he can't even lose a game
rry! without sinning, how will he handle real
pointment when it comes? Help him find a way

to bless someone who has cursed him. As he changes, his countenance will be lifted up.

"He must increase, and I must decrease": John the Baptist knew what the too-big person does not. If you demand love, respect, and significance, you will by no means get it. Do you want those things enough to get them God's way?

That's a trick question, because if you use God to get them, you still won't. He must increase, remember? He's not your butler, He's the sovereign Lord of the universe. If you have a worship disorder, you have no fear of God before your eyes and it would be cruel of Him to bless your desires. Your soul's health depends on your moving back into the love and kindness of our good God.

In what ways do you need to repent today? To increasingly have eyes to see (even if what you see in yourself is painful), ears to hear (even though you may want to plug them back up!), and a heart that understands is the beginning of true freedom in Christ.

e friends with your conscience and you will have ity to be unspeakably glad that you did.

will be especially true if you have married into a ly where your spouse and your in-laws are ptionally difficult, and you don't have anyone to you. Pray fervently for human help, but in the ntime, the Lord will lead you by His own hand if keep a quiet soul. One of the clearest messages the of 1 Peter communicates is that you are not free to ond however you wish when you are suffering stly. This is true of every single believer. You are our own; you have been bought with the precious d of Christ. Therefore, you must follow Him and r Him when you suffer. Remember, dear brother ister in Christ, that the Lord never removes hing, including the help of other believers, except ve His child more of Himself. If He has seemingly ou alone, trust Jesus to meet you where you are. ll chapter 6, in which I mentioned the satanic ent in this type of persecution, and also remember that it is impossible for the enemy to triumph over God's child.

For this is a gracious thing, when, mindful of God, one endures sorrows while suffering unjustly. For what credit is it if, when you sin and are beaten for it, you endure? But if when you do good and suffer for it you endure, this is a gracious thing in the sight of God. For to this you have been called, because Christ also suffered for you, leaving you an example, so that you might follow in his steps. He committed no sin, neither was deceit found in his mouth. When he was reviled, he did not revile in return; when he suffered, he did not threaten, but continued entrusting himself to him who judges justly. He himself bore our sins in his body on the tree, that we might die to sin and live to righteousness. By his wounds you have been healed. For you were straying like sheep, but have now returned to the Shepherd and Overseer of your souls.

1 Peter 2:19–25

Likewise, wives, be subject to your own husbands, so that even if some do not obey the word, they may be won without a word by the conduct of their wives, when they see your respectful and pure conduct. Do not let your adorning be external—the braiding of hair and the putting on of gold jewelry, or the clothing you wear—but let your adorning be the hidden person of the heart with the imperishable beauty of a gentle and quiet spirit, which in God's sight is very precious.

I etting up our final case study, I'm focusing p cularly on wives who are being treated harshly, b you will, I trust, be able to make application to a v ty of circumstances as you consider the example o ır fictional couple.

T call to win a harsh husband without a word does n nean you will never speak to him, nor does it mean t you will never rebuke him. What this passage n ıs is that if you give yourself permission to revile y husband (or anyone) in response to his reviling, o you try to nag him into repentance, you will be h ering what the Spirit would do in and through you i u responded otherwise. This is not by any means a c o be a doormat; steadfastness, wisdom, courage, a humility, are tremendously powerful tools to c ɔat the evil in your family.

sider Abigail in 1 Samuel 25. She is called c rning and beautiful, while her husband is described as worthless and badly behaved. Abigail chose to go against Nabal's wishes, described him as being worthless (telling the truth, which is crucial, and can and must be done without reviling), and put her own life in danger for his best interests. King David or Nabal could have killed her for her impudence, but she did the right thing, trusting YHWH with the results. If she had time to prepare a feast for David and his men, she surely could have gathered supplies for herself and her faithful servants who had looked to her for leadership and fled to safety. No one legitimately could have faulted her for leaving the wicked man to the end he earned for himself. She chose, however, to serve the foolish men in her life in humility and grace. This woman was not a doormat, and she was not passive. She obviously had spent years putting her selfishness to death so that she was neither needy nor greedy, and so she acted in power and freedom when her household faced its greatest danger.

I ›w several women like Abigail, and they are among r ıeroes. This book, more than for anyone else, is for t ı and for the others like them whom I will never ı . The world is not worthy of any believer who s rs righteously, and I think that's doubly true of v ıen who are abandoned by everyone who should h protected them, and who choose to make much of (st through their torment and tears. The Lord sees y my sisters. My daughters. Do not grow weary, for Y VH fights for you.

I u are seeking to help a lady in this type of marriage a family situation, do not assume she is equally to b e for the problems. It will take patience, prayer, v om, and discernment to see to what degree she is h ble and willing to be led, or whether she is tearing h amily down with her own hands, just as much as h husband is. Either or both spouses could be c ptive and manipulative—if you've seen one case l his, you've seen…one case like this. The dynamics c ch family are different, even though you may well notice Saul-like characteristics in either person. If you've seen a marriage where, say, the wife is the primary problem, don't let that cause you to assume this will always be the case. She may well be a David or an Abigail and in desperate need of your help.

Yes, it's hard. Yes, it's confusing. The enemy wants you to throw your hands up and back off, which is why he is so relentless. You will make mistakes in your care, but as long as you're humble and willing to learn, sturdy and growing in wisdom, the Lord will bless your efforts. The only available alternative to helping, in whatever ways you are willing and capable of doing, is to aid the enemy's and the demigod's deception and fail to challenge their claims to power. Nobody sane actually wants that responsibility, and few will take it on. If you are in the position of needing help that you are not getting from human sources, be gracious as you consider how daunting a task it is to help you. You most likely wouldn't understand it either, were you not experiencing it. Be patient, be gracious, be willing to

t ı and to forgive. Don't do anything that would be
h ıful to your family and yourself in order to appease
s ›one's misguided views of grace or forgiveness,
a don't revile anyone for being clueless. You may
c se to distance yourself from clueless people, but if
y look down on them for what they don't
u ›rstand, the enemy will be well on his way to
i encing you to be a demigod in your own right.

T is a hard road, but it's the one the Lord uses to
r › leaders, should they want the job. What makes it
e more difficult is that the best leaders don't lust
a position or influence—they would be most
c ›nt to live a quiet life of service, extending and
r ving faithfulness and kindness. Being a humble
s herd boy, ala David, who was chosen by God for
y ; of Satanic persecution until he had died to
h elf, makes the only kind of king worth having. You
r never be king or queen, but your sphere of
i ence needs exactly who you will be if you allow

suffering and perseverance to have their perfect work in you.

11

Case Study 3: Joan

And he in all his glory
Was far ahead of her
But she was never sorry
For wishes that would burn
Enter competition
She chases beneath the moon
Her horse is like a dragonfly
She is just a fool

And she wonders, is this real?
Or does she just want to be queen?
And he fights the way he feels
Is this the end of a dream?

And then he sees her coming
Heartbeats on the wind
Considers slowing down
But then he could never win
And she out in the distance
Sees him against the sky
A pale and violent rider
A dream begun in wine

Stevie Nicks

"We're so encouraged that you both are here, willing to work on your marriage." The counselor smiled kindly.

His wife sat next to him, looking joyful and radiant. She loved her husband; you could tell just by looking at her. She wanted Donny and Joan to have what she had. She introduced herself, and expressed her optimism and her firm hope that they were on their way to a great marriage because she knew her God. Nothing was impossible for Him. Nothing.

She's already written a Hallmark movie ending for us, Joan thought. *Lord, please help me love this woman, your child. Please help me.*

"It means a lot to us that you are willing to serve us in this way." Donny had a sober look on his movie star face. He glanced at the counselor's wife and gave her the quickest of winks before returning his full attention to the counselor. Immediately, Joan could see that the wink had had its desired effect, and her heart sank.

T man asked them to share what brought them into
t ounseling office that day, so Donny went first. He
r inted fifteen difficult years of marriage, and made
r ence to their unsuccessful efforts to get help at
t previous church.

" wife has been telling me all these years that the
p lems in our marriage are all my fault, and I finally
b ve her." A pained look of shock passed over the
f of the counselor's wife. She looked back and forth
b een Donny and Joan, trying to discern whether
J actually thought she had nothing to do with the
c le's issues. "No, really, they are. I have been the
w t of husbands. I used to have a porn problem, and
I had a few emotional affairs as well. My dad was
a ngry man, and I can fly off the handle sometimes,
t Over the past two years, since our previous elders
c ronted me, I have been trying to do better. I'm not
c ging overnight; I mean, I've been this way my
w le life, so I'm not perfect, but I'm trying. I think that

my wife was just so hurt by me in the past that she's having a hard time giving me grace now."

"Your elders did reach out to us and share a bit of their perspectives regarding your marriage. Tell us about your interactions with them, from your point of view."

As Joan watched Donny speak, she tried to listen to him as if she had never met him before. His huge brown eyes looked like a little boy's, lost and earnest, as he recounted all of the ways their pastors had sided with her, ganging up on him. What person wouldn't believe him? She still believed him, way too often. "I don't want to disparage them at all. I know they were trying to do their best." *Vintage Donny,* she thought. What he wasn't saying was that Donny himself had controlled the elders' perceptions of the couple, right up until the final two months they attended the church. They only started to believe Joan at the end, and even then they were charitable to Donny.

Both the counselor and his wife turned their heads to look at Joan. Did the warmth of their expressions cool uch, just in that moment? Joan couldn't be lutely sure. She swallowed hard. She thought t all of these long, hard years alone, living with a for whom the world was a stage, and before whom doring fans fawned. *Hypocrite,* she thought. *That's actors used to be called. Pretending to be someone they ot.* Except that on a real stage, everyone knows it's an act. Just as she had glimpsed her first bit of that someone may at last help her, Donny had a job in another town to move their family away the people who were starting to see who he really *Oh, God, I can't do this again. Please.*

ever had hit her. In fact, Donny had very strong ls for anyone who would hit a woman. This, like everything else he said and did, made women on. *You are so blessed, Joan,* they would say. She ld smile and say nothing because, well, what could ay? She didn't want to agree and help him lie, and lidn't want to air their junk in that context. She would end up looking like the jerk anyway, and Donny would come out smelling like a rose.

He never hit her, but he would break her things. Why did he never break his own things when he was angry? He would berate the kids, her precious kids, when he was mad, as a way to punish her. Her dog was a nervous wreck because anything and anyone she cared about was a potential weapon to be used against her. If she spoke up, he accused her of being disrespectful. If she ever got angry or cried, he cried, too, and asked why it was ok for her to get angry, but it wasn't ok for him. When they had a disagreement, which was anytime Donny didn't get his way, he would lecture her for hours, even well into the early morning, not letting her sleep "until we get this thing resolved." Why, he demanded, was she always trying to run from their problems? She had learned long ago just to give in, earlier rather than later. It wasn't worth it; she would never win.

I ıblic, he talked about how much he loved Joan, and j 1 about what a lout he was. This, of course, drew g natured objections from their friends. Joan was e usted, and she felt crazy.

I ıy's version of doing better the past few years was t extra nice the day before a counseling session, p ımably because he knew that Joan's integrity v ld require her to report his good behavior. Until r ıtly, she had been afraid to communicate her s ticism about his motives because Donny used to be a to persuade their pastors that nothing he could e do, no matter how good, would ever satisfy Joan. T truth, in fact, was the exact opposite: Joan had s t years running herself ragged trying to serve a r who refused to be pleased. When they weren't in c seling, Donny gave up any pretense of trying to i ove himself.

" ı, it's good to meet you," the counselor's wife b n. She was smiling, but her eyes were firm. "I'm s your marriage has been such a struggle, and that your pastors were unable to help you. Will you please tell us your side of the story? I'm particularly interested in the ways you've contributed to the problems. No conflict is solely the fault of one person, as you know. Please help us know and understand you better." Donnie made eye contact with Joan, and she could read the subtle expression of triumph in his face.

I can't lie; I can't help Donny lie. I can't bear any more pressure to do better. God, what am I supposed to do?

For the two-dozenth time, she thought of her brother's offer to take her and the kids in. He and Joan had lived with their single mother's tantrums and control for years, and he wanted to help her now. Michael was a committed believer and had the support of his elders to act as Joan's stand-in father, to care for Joan's soul and to make Donny answer to him and them about his sin against his family—the precious wife and kids God had given him to protect. Joan had never felt much worth protecting, and she was well used to ill treatment, but she didn't want her kids to grow up feeling that way.

wanted her marriage to work, and she took her seriously, so the decision was incredibly difficult. vouldn't have been sad if Donny had run off with ıer woman, but she would not be the one to break ›romise to the Lord.

ong as no one holds him accountable, Joan, Donny has eason to change. He thinks he is a god, and that he can hatever he wants to. I want to stand between him and I want his good. I want him to succeed. I intend to do hat's right for all of you. Please think about it. Your ulders are too small to bear all of this by yourself. The d will sustain you if you stay, but maybe you leaving be what brings him to repentance. Even if it doesn't, an have a break and some time to start thinking clearly ı. The men and I can help you decide when a good time l be for your return, as we care for Donny, too, if he's willing to receive care.

never could remember what she said to the selor and his wife that day. They were good le, and she hoped that the Lord would continue to them, but she needed help that they could not ide. That evening, when Donny left to play softball his friends, Joan called Michael.

12

Conclusion

Did they get you to trade your heroes for ghosts?

Hot ashes for trees?

Hot air for a cool breeze?

Cold comfort for change?

Did you exchange a walk-on part in the war for a lead role in a cage?

Pink Floyd

In chapter 3, I mentioned that people who think too highly of themselves may see you as the small person in the graphic, the dark, insignificant one at the end of the line. I went on to say that agreeing with them will be your secret weapon in living with and serving someone like this, but I think there's more to say on the matter. There's another element to the graphic that your eye can't see: a grain of salt.

M nentor, Rick Thomas from the ministry Life Over C ee, once recounted a counseling session he had c breakfast at a restaurant. The couple he was c seling was in a difficult situation in which the lady v being treated unfairly. During the course of the c ersation, Rick took the lid off the salt shaker on t table and spilled its contents, and he asked his f ds to imagine that the grains of salt were the E tian army pursuing the Israelites to the Red Sea in t ook of Exodus. He then pointed out one tiny grain, r senting a soldier who would soon be drowned, a asked the lady to imagine that she was his wife.

T wife of the man represented by the grain of salt was i nately connected to one of the most important e ts of human history. In drowning the Egyptian a , the Lord was preserving the line of His promised M siah, eventually making a way for lost people to be r red to Himself. No one knows that woman's r e, but the Egyptian lady could have chosen to s e her fist at the God who parted the sea and drowned her husband. She, too, could have turned to God, thanking Him for sparing her life and asking Him to save her soul if she had the wisdom and humility to do so. The Lord had revealed Himself to Egypt in His infinite might, and the sane response of any person would have been to see herself as a grain of salt in comparison to His righteousness and grandeur, and to surrender in worship. It wasn't about her, it was about YHWH, His glory, and His people, and she had a small but privileged part to play in His narrative if she would refuse to make it about herself and her own suffering, as significant as her suffering was.

Pharaoh, like King Saul and King Nebuchadnezzar, was a symbol of the satanic persecution of God's people that still continues today. He is the large, three headed demigod in our graphic, believing that he is the be all, end all of the universe. But who are you, dear reader? Do you know that all of history is about God and *His* plans and purposes, and that your part in it is at the same time tiny and tremendously significant? Are you c ent with being a grain of salt, not lofty in your own e but faithful to the Lord? If you are, He may well u you in ways that far exceed what you can possibly i gine.

A who desire to live godly lives in Christ will be p ecuted, while evil people and impostors will go on f bad to worse, deceiving and being deceived (2 T othy 3:12). So it will be until Christ returns and sets a hings right. As I've mentioned before, it will often l like our enemy is winning, but nothing could be f her from the truth. One little word, as Martin L er said, shall fell him.

I ve counseled many too-big people, and I've also c seled many folks seeking to live with demigods as b they can. My desire in writing this is to provide s help to those who have no idea where to start, a no idea what's appropriate care and what is not. I p that you, the people you serve, and the people l ing to serve you will be helped by my words. The L gives grace to the humble, and so His very hand will complete what is lacking in my care for you if you pursue Him in courage, humility, and utter dependence upon Christ.

If in reading this you have been convicted that you are characterized by self-worship and lording over others, there is hope for you in Christ. Sometimes Christians can and do live this way, no doubt, but I would encourage you to consider whether you truly are His if you have chosen to live an utterly selfish life. If you believe you are indeed saved, cry out to Him night and day for repentance and for help in bearing His image more fully.

If, though, you realize that your life is earthly, unspiritual, and demonic because you have never been born again, repent and trust in Christ now for the forgiveness of your sins. Do you remember how I described myself in the introduction to this book? It was easy for me to see, by God's Spirit, that I needed a Savior because my sin was so huge, and it was ever before me. Do you see *your* need, my friend? The Bible that God is of purer eyes than to look upon evil. oesn't just possess truth, goodness, and beauty, He uth, Goodness, and Beauty, and any violation of character is an infinite offense against a perfectly and Holy God. An evil judge knowingly lets the y go free, but God is a perfectly good and eous judge and **no** sin, not even one, goes unished with Him.

e God who is Truth itself, any lie makes the liar hy of the lake of fire for all eternity. And not just ig lies: even things like exaggeration, flattery, and telling the whole truth are very serious. Jesus self said in John 8 that those who lie have the devil eir father, as do those who murder. Is that you? you a liar?

may be thinking that you have never murdered ne, but did you know that Jesus also said that if disdain someone, you are guilty of murdering in your heart? Even if someone genuinely is bad has sinned against you grievously, you cannot murder them in your heart without being guilty before God. Whom do you hate? Liberals? Conservatives? Racists? Mine is cowards—I have to guard against murdering cowards in my heart. Why? Because I'm not a coward and I think I'm better than they are, so I tend to hate them. When I do that, I'm guilty of murdering in my heart, and I desperately need the Lord's forgiveness. Do you hate Millennials? Boomers? Smug gen-x'ers? Do slow or dumb drivers make you cuss? You are a murderer at heart, Friend.

Jesus said that if you lust after someone, you are guilty of adultery, which is a violation of the seventh commandment. Marriage is a picture of Christ and His faithfulness to His church, and He cannot let adultery or any other mockery of marriage go without being unfaithful to Himself, which He cannot do. Are you an adulterer?

I hope you feel the weight of what I'm saying, because if you do, it will make hearing of Christ infinitely sweet.

owe a debt you cannot pay. An eternity in hell d never satisfy the righteous requirement of God, He would be just to condemn us all, but He loves people so much that He sent His Son so that yone who would repent and put their faith in Him d be ***completely forgiven.*** You can be clean!!

n, He cannot pardon the guilty, so let me tell you He can forgive you. The first Adam--and all of kind--failed, so the Holy Spirit created another n, a rational human soul and body in the womb of y. A rational human soul and body cannot exist out being the rational human soul and body OF eone, so the second person of the Trinity, the very of God, supplied a who to the what, so that the st was not only a new representative for fallen , but He also was and is Yahweh Himself-- dless love, goodness, worth, and perfection, and use of this, only His sacrifice could satisfy the ite debt His people owed. He is true man and ite, holy God, in one person, and He died a death

He did not deserve for YOU, if you will repent and trust Him.

The Father placed the sin of everyone who would ever come to Christ on Him, and punished Him in our place, which makes me--and hopefully you--not guilty. Even better, though, Jesus kept the Law perfectly, and when you trust Him, not only is your sin paid for but you also get His perfect obedience credited to you, so that when the Father sees you on Judgment Day, He won't see your filthy record; He will see the sinless perfection of His dear Son, credited to you.

Jesus rose from the dead, defeating sin and death once for all, and He sits at the right hand of the Father now praying for His people. He will return one day, not as the Lamb of God who takes away the sin of the world, but as the Lion of the Tribe of Judah. If your knee does not bow to Him now, it will then, and my friend, it will not go well for you if that is the case.

I live in a small town, full of salt of the earth folks who are good neighbors, but many are still blind to the

c ns on their souls. When you go to a small-town
(rado funeral, the pastor or whoever is officiating is
s om faithful to Christ, and seldom is faithful to the
s of the people listening. As long as nothing has
g horribly wrong in a person's life, or even if it HAS,
s y, most will assure their listeners that their loved
c s in a better place when it's usually not true. Jesus
I self said that few would be saved, not many, and
c inly not most.

I earlier chapter, we considered the faithfulness of
I d. As good as King David was, even he was not
g l enough to stand before God on his own merit. He
r ed *and he has had* his sin removed and the very
r eousness of the Son of God credited to him.
N ody is guaranteed tomorrow and your funeral
c l be one week from today. Jesus stands ready to
s you. Will you turn from your sin and put your
t in Christ alone?

I you who have come to worship Christ in His
g deur and have embraced your own grain-of-

saltness, remember that you are precious to the Lord. It looks and feels at times like you are being defeated, but it is in fact impossible for you to be overcome because of whose you are. Do not trust in what your eyes see, to the exclusion of God's promises. He will return soon, and your faithfulness will be lavishly rewarded, even as He crushes His (and your) enemies under His feet. You will be infinitely and eternally glad on that day for every act of loving obedience, and also for everything you have suffered for His sake.

It's worth it, Friend; do not grow weary. Everyone suffers in this life, and I want you to suffer with Christ, not in opposition to Him. It's counterintuitive, I know, but this is the way of freedom and joy. The reputation of the *a se,* impassible God hangs on the unchangeableness of His Word, and thus it cannot fail. You are in union with the Son, and so the Father's perfect love for Christ is yours as well. He can't forsake you any more than He can forsake Jesus. Love God, love your enemies, and keep a quiet soul. Do not lie to self, ever, and don't help others lie either. Don't yourself permission to return evil for evil, even in heart. Plunder the resources I cited in this book. ound yourself with God's people, avail yourself of love and help, and as you do so, I pray that my will be a gift to you.

Did we in our own strength confide
Our striving would be losing
We're not the right Man on our side
The Man of God's own choosing
Dost ask who that may be?
Christ Jesus, it is He
Lord Sabaoth His Name
From age to age, the same
And He must win the battle

That word above all earthly powers
No, thanks to them, abideth
The Spirit and the gifts are ours
Through Him who with us sideth
Let goods and kindred go
This mortal life also
The body they may kill
God's truth abideth still
His Kingdom is forever

From *A Mighty Fortress is Our God*, by Martin Luther

Yours in Christ,

Brandi Huerta

Brandih190@yahoo.com